All About
MARKET
INDICATORS

MICHAEL SINCERE

New York   Chicago   San Francisco   Lisbon   London
Madrid   Mexico City   Milan   New Delhi   San Juan
Seoul   Singapore   Sydney   Toronto

1 2 3 4 5 6 7 8 9 10   DOC/DOC   1 9 8 7 6 5 4 3 2 1 0

ISBN   978-0-07-174884-1
MHID   0-07-174884-9

This publication is designed to provide accurate and authoritative information in regard to the subject matter covered. It is sold with the understanding that neither the author nor the publisher is engaged in rendering legal, accounting, securities trading, or other professional services. If legal advice or other expert assistance is required, the services of a competent professional person should be sought.

—*From a Declaration of Principles Jointly Adopted by*
a Committee of the American Bar Association and
a Committee of Publishers and Associations

Trademarks: McGraw-Hill, the McGraw-Hill Publishing logo, All About, and related trade dress are trademarks or registered trademarks of The McGraw-Hill Companies and/or its affiliates in the United States and other countries and may not be used without written permission. All other trademarks are the property of their respective owners. The McGraw-Hill Companies is not associated with any product or vendor mentioned in this book.

McGraw-Hill books are available at special quantity discounts to use as premiums and sales promotions or for use in corporate training programs. To contact a representative, please e-mail us at bulksales@mcgraw-hill.com.

This book is printed on acid-free paper.

* * * * *

To my amazing mother, Lois, who asked for so little, but accomplished so much—I miss the unique way she viewed the world.

* * * * *

CONTENTS

PART THREE: UNDERSTANDING VOLUME

PART FOUR: ONE STEP BEYOND

Every Indicator Tells a Story

WHAT'S THE MARKET GOING TO DO NEXT?

Why did professional trader and Market Wizard Linda Raschke move completely out of the stock market three days before a major crash? And what motivated Fred Hickey, a *Barron's* Roundtable participant and editor of a monthly investment newsletter, to send out an alert to his subscribers three months before an October crash? And why did economist Bernard Baumohl recommend going long in the midst of one of the greatest recessions since the Great Depression?

Is it luck or is it really possible to forecast what the market will do next? By the time you finish *All About Market Indicators*, you'll have an answer.

In this book, you'll be taking an entertaining and educational journey. Along the way, you'll meet a lot of fascinating people with different opinions about how to use market indicators. Some of the people you'll meet use indicators to trade and invest, others create their own, and many do both. I've included an all-star lineup of experts willing to share their knowledge and insights. I'm sure you won't be disappointed.

Fortunately, you won't need an advanced degree in mathematics, psychology, or economics to use these indicators. As I said in my previous book, *Understanding Options*, you don't need to know how an engine is built to drive a car. It's the same with market indicators. Although a few of the indicators have been built using complicated algorithms, most are easier to use than driving a car. In fact, some of the most reliable indicators are the simplest. With that in mind, let's keep our focus on the main goal: to help you make or protect money by learning how to properly use market indicators.

A note to experienced traders: This book is different from other books written about the stock market. If you're looking for traditional trading books with dozens of signals, look in Chapter 12 for suggestions. My book is aimed at helping traders and investors who are unfamiliar with market indicators quickly get started. In addition, which is why this book is so different, I've included dozens of interviews with experts who shared their insights about trading with indicators. I believe you'll find the interviews invaluable.

If You're New to the Stock Market

If you're an emerging trader or investor, let me explain what I mean by the market, a word you'll hear a lot in this book. The "market" refers to a major financial index. The three major stock market indexes are the Dow Jones Industrial Average (Symbol: $DJI, .DJI, or ^DJI), the Nasdaq Composite (Symbol: $COMPQ, .IXIC, or ^IXIC), and the Standard & Poor's 500 (S&P 500) Index (Symbol: $SPX, .INX, or ^GSPC). Because the S&P 500 represents such a broad spectrum of stocks, in this book, this is the market I'm usually referring to. (Note: The symbol for these indexes will vary, depending on the chart program you use.)

You might wonder how it's possible to buy or sell any of these three indexes. The answer? If you want to trade stocks in the Dow Jones, for example, you can trade an exchange-traded fund (ETF) with the symbol DIA (nicknamed the Diamonds). If you want to trade the stocks in the Nasdaq, you can trade an ETF with the symbol QQQQ (nicknamed the Cubes). And if you want to trade the stocks in the S&P 500, you can trade an ETF with the symbol SPY (nicknamed the Spyders).

A PSYCHOLOGICAL BATTLEFIELD

The stock market is a psychological battlefield, and if you're going to participate, you'd better bring a set of powerful tools, especially market indicators. The indicators can be technical, sentiment, or economic, but their purpose is to give you insights into market direction. Just as a carpenter needs a hammer to build a house and a golfer needs the best clubs, traders and investors need market indicators.

You're not only battling other buyers and sellers but also your own raw emotions. And for that, you need an unbiased and unemotional source that can keep you on the right side of the market. Using market indicators can keep your emotions in check and allow you to focus on the facts. The market is not only a psychological battlefield but also a huge mind game. Using indicators can help you keep your mind focused on the game.

Market indicators can do even more. When used properly, market indicators can act as an early warning system, alerting you to potentially dangerous market conditions, or signaling when it's safe to buy again. Many traders use indicators to determine when buyers have become too greedy or fearful. Indicators can also identify when the market or an individual stock might reverse direction.

In addition, many traders simply use indicators to monitor market conditions, especially the current market trend: up, down, or sideways. For all of these reasons, using market indicators makes sense.

Finally, to make profitable buying and selling decisions, you need up-to-date and correct information, and that's how market indicators can help. What you hear on television or read in the news can often be misleading. After a severe market correction, tons of articles appear in the papers that predict the market will fall even more. And then, if you look at the indicators, they might say the exact opposite. Whom do you believe?

It would be nice if someone rang a bell to signal which way the financial winds were blowing. Since this bell doesn't exist, we have to rely on tools, such as . . . you guessed it: market indicators.

TRADING FOR A LIFETIME

Another reason you should use market indicators is to help choose individual stocks. According to research, more than 75 percent of stocks follow the market. Therefore, using indicators to anticipate the market's direction could improve your stock performance. They help put the odds, and potential profits, on your side.

Using indicators means you no longer have to rely on some blowhard on TV, or your neighbors, to tell you what stocks to buy or sell. Listen to them—and you'll probably spend years trying to get back to even.

It's really quite simple: If you receive stock tips from other people, you'll trade for a day. But if you learn to find your own stocks using market indicators, you'll trade for a lifetime.

HOW THE BOOK IS ORGANIZED

All About Market Indicators is unique because while half of the book helps you learn how to use indicators, the other half takes you directly into the minds of professional traders and investors. Even more exciting, at the end of each section, I include a profile with an indicator creator. Charts of their indicators are included in Chapter 12.

This book is organized into four parts. Part One, "The Most Popular Market Indicators," introduces popular indicators that have stood the test of time. With this wide assortment of indicators, you should be able to examine almost any market environment.

Part Two, "How Traders Anticipate Market Direction," is another must-read. In this section you'll find out how professional traders use various methods to trade the stock market. More than likely, you'll learn something new.

Part Three, "Understanding Volume," introduces volume basics but also describes how high-frequency trading (HFT) is changing all the rules.

Part Four, "One Step Beyond," is the final wrap-up. As a special treat, you'll also learn what to do in case of a market emergency. In addition, after interviewing the experts, doing the research, and using the indicators, I'll briefly summarize what I have learned. Finally, this section is loaded with important resources such as where to get help, additional charts, backtest ideas, and a glossary of indicators.

Suggestion: Like most of my books, it will seem short, but it's packed with information. Therefore, it's probably best to go slowly and try not to learn all of the indicators in only one reading. That being said, I set up the book so you can start immediately.

READ INDICATORS IN FIVE MINUTES

Perhaps the biggest surprise is that it takes less than five minutes to set up most market indicators. Five minutes? Yes, it's usually quite easy to set up a market indicator on a chart. The hard part is correctly interpreting what you see.

After all, thousands of people are looking at the same indicators that you are, but everyone may see them differently. Although teaching you how to use indicators will be relatively easy, your learning how to turn the results into profitable trades will be a challenge.

ALL SIGNALS ARE GO!

All About Market Indicators was written for everybody who participates in the stock market or is thinking of doing so. It doesn't matter if you're a trader, investor, or saver, learning how to anticipate the next bull or bear market, or a possible crash, is necessary for financial survival.

By the end of the book, you'll be able to set up market indicators within minutes and use them to give you an unbiased, unemotional view of the market. They will also help you see the bigger picture.

If you finish the book with a different view of this entity we call the stock market, then I've achieved my goals. Although there are no guarantees that any of the indicators in the book will lead you to unimagined riches, I can guarantee you a good read.

It is hoped that you keep an open mind about what you'll learn. Choosing an indicator is like choosing your favorite food. Some like Italian, some Thai, and others like American. You can't say one is better than the other. There is no one-size-fits-all indicator.

It's a personal decision, and by the time you've finished, you'll have a better idea what works for you.

Although there are a dozen reasons why you'd use market indicators, perhaps the most important is this: The next time some-one asks you, "What's the market going to do next?" you know what to do—hand over a copy of my book!

I hope you have a good time. I'll have more to say later.

WHAT'S NEXT?

You'll learn that every indicator has a distinctive personality and a "story to tell" (thanks to author Michael Kahn for coming up with the phrase). Throughout Part One, you'll read about the most pop-ular market indicators and the stories they have to tell.

The Most Popular Market Indicators

THE MOST POWERFUL INDICATOR IN THE WORLD

There is one indicator that is more powerful than all the others. Without a doubt, this indicator has the final word. That indicator is the market itself, represented by any of the major indexes, including the Dow Jones Industrial Average, Nasdaq, S&P 500, Russell 2000, or Wilshire 5000, to name the most popular.

The best way to show you is by looking at the chart below of the S&P 500 (SPX) with a three-year time period.

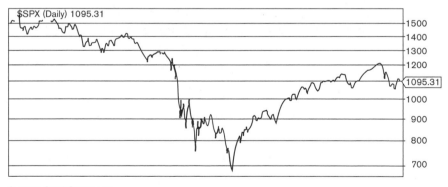

Source: StockCharts.com

If you like to keep things simple, but not too simple, then buy stocks when the line is moving up (also referred to as an *uptrend*) or sell stocks when the line is moving down (also referred to as a *downtrend*). People have made fortunes following this uncomplicated but reliable strategy of following the market trend.

You might wonder why you need other indicators, since the market itself tells you so much. In fact, many people believe that everything you need to know about a stock is found in the chart. And for some people, this is as far as they go, and that's fine.

Nevertheless, if you want to gain more insights into the market, you'll want to add indicators to this chart. Then you'll see for yourself how interesting the stock market can get.

Note: In all of the charts in this book, line charts are used because they are so easy to read. But in the real trading environment, you'll probably want to use candlestick charts because they give more detailed information.

WHAT'S NEXT?

Although dozens of indicators are discussed in this book, including more in Chapter 12, I'm going to introduce you to the most popular market indicators. If you've never used a chart before, you're in the right place.

Since you already know that every indicator tells a story, I had a little fun by giving each indicator its own nickname and personality. Ready? Let's get started learning about the first set of indicators, which are appropriately named "Reverse Psychology."

CHAPTER 1

Reverse Psychology

The more you study the stock market, the more you'll realize it's fueled by the fear, greed, and hope of millions of market participants. So it should not be surprising that the market indicators in this chapter are used to monitor what the crowd is feeling.

These indicators are perhaps the easiest to read and understand, but they can give you the most revealing clues, especially at market extremes. Knowing when the crowds are panicked or overconfident is essential if you are going to enter the market. The stock market is psychological warfare, and you'd better know what others are thinking before you enter.

The following indicators are commonly referred to as sentiment indicators because they monitor the sentiment, or psychology, of the market. And as you'll soon find out, it's an Alice in Wonderland kind of world, where up is down and down is up.

Traders and investors closely follow the first indicator, the AAII Sentiment Survey.

AMERICAN ASSOCIATION OF INDIVIDUAL INVESTORS

"little guys"

Name: American Association of Individual Investors (AAII)

Where to find: www.aaii.com/sentimentsurvey, *Barron's*, *Forbes*, and other financial periodicals

Time period: Weekly survey

The Lighter Side: The AAII Sentiment Survey, which I nicknamed "The Little Guy," will keep you out of trouble when the markets get extreme. A little secret: do the opposite of the little guy.

WHAT AAII DOES

AAII polls their members via the Internet to find out how the members feel the stock market will do over the next six months: bullish, bearish, or neutral.

HOW TO READ AAII IN FIVE MINUTES

Go to www.aaii.com/sentimentsurvey to read the survey results. It will look something like Figure 1.1.

FIGURE 1.1

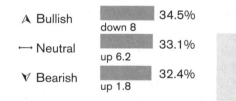

⋏ Bullish	34.5% down 8	AAII's members were asked to finish this sentence:
⟷ Neutral	33.1% up 6.2	*"I feel that the direction of the stock market over the next six months will be:* ***Bearish, Neutral,*** *or* ***Bullish."***
⋎ Bearish	32.4% up 1.8	

Summary — "This week's survey saw bullish sentiment rise to **34.5%**, below its long-term average of 38.9%. Neutral sentiment rose to **33.1%**. below the long-term average of 31.1%. And bearish sentiment fell to **32.4%** above the long-term average of 30.0%."

Change from Last Week:

Bullish: **−8.0**

Neutral: **+6.2**

Bearish: **+1.8**

Long-Term Average:

Bullish: **39%**

Neutral: **31%**

Bearish: **30%**

Source: American Association of Individual Investors (AAII)

WHAT SIGNALS TO LOOK FOR

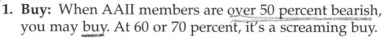

1. **Buy:** When AAII members are over 50 percent bearish, you may buy. At 60 or 70 percent, it's a screaming buy.
2. **Sell:** When AAII members are over 60 percent bullish, you may sell. At 70 percent, it's a screaming sell.
3. **Note:** These are not actionable trades, but only guidelines. Always use other indicators to confirm before buying or selling.

THE BACK STORY

AAII is a nonprofit educational organization founded in 1978 by James Cloonan. Members are typically nearing or in retirement and have a relatively high net worth. One of the organization's goals is to educate individual investors to manage their own portfolios.

In 1987, AAII started polling individual members each week about the stock market. Before the Internet, random AAII members were polled by postcards; since 2000, all members have to do is vote online.

It wasn't long before the financial world discovered that the poll results could be used as a contrarian indicator. In other words, if members are feeling excessively bullish or bearish, traders could do well by doing the exact opposite.

WHY THE AAII SURVEY WORKS

There is nothing more fascinating than getting inside the heads of individual investors. After all, the market is driven by twin emotions of fear and greed, as pointed out by traders such as Jesse Livermore or investors such as Warren Buffett.

Therefore, it is not surprising that one of the most watched is the weekly AAII Sentiment Survey. The results are published on the AAII Web site or in financial periodicals such as *Barron's* and give insights into the mind of the little guy. At times, the survey can be uncannily accurate—that is, it can be if you do the opposite of what the members are feeling.

"The survey gets interesting when we see levels of excess," says Charles Rotblut, vice president and *AAII Journal* editor. "It might not be the exact bottom but that first high reading is a definite sign you should be looking for confirmation. In other words, look for additional signs to support your contrarian belief, such as valuation, changes in earnings estimates, and chart formations."

If you graph the results on a chart, says Rotblut, you are looking for results that are at least two standard deviations away from the mean. One standard deviation would be on the outer edge of normal. Two standard deviations and members are feeling either scared they'll lose their portfolio or giddy by how much money they're making. At three standard deviations, the survey really shines. For example, one of the highest readings of all time was 70 percent bearishness. The following year, the market zoomed up over 80 percent.

Typically, says Wayne Thorp, senior financial analyst of AAII and editor of *Computerized Investing*, "when you start hitting 60 percent sentiment on the bearish or bullish side, your ears should perk up."

Historically, that means the market is hitting an extreme. "I think over the short term the market is completely driven by sentiment," Thorp cautions. "In case of extremes, the fundamentals tend to go out the window."

The survey seems to work as a contrarian indicator because it's not just the members who are feeling extreme emotion but also the majority of the people in the stock market. And yet, it's hard to do the opposite of how you feel.

"At a certain point," Rotblut explains, "members succumb to irrational exuberance or are overwrought with fear about what is going on in the markets. The hardest thing for someone to do is to buy low and sell high, even though study after study shows that you should be greedy when others are fearful and fearful when others are greedy, to paraphrase Warren Buffett. When you're looking at the balance of your account plummeting, or you're looking at it jumping in value, it's really hard to take a stand against the tide. It's human emotion."

One suggestion from Rotblut is that during the next bull market, write down what you will do in the next bear market. "When people are not under stress, they make rational decisions. But when they are under stress, they tend to make irrational decisions. They let their emotions take over."

It's hard to step in and buy when you're losing money in the middle of a bear market, he says. "From an emotional standpoint, it's extremely hard to do. From a financial standpoint, it's often the best move you can make."

NOBODY'S PERFECT

The AAII survey is often eerily accurate, capturing extreme pessimism or panic precisely at the exact bottom, or overconfidence at the very top. But in the months between the two extremes, you might not learn much. Technically, the sentiment survey was not designed as a timing indicator, but many have tried to use it that way.

Even if you do use the survey to try to time tops or bottoms, more than likely, you'll be early. So perhaps the only criticism is that although it does work at tops and bottoms, it's only one piece of the puzzle. When the numbers get high in either direction, you take notice, but you don't run out and trade based on the survey's results.

WHAT'S NEXT?

Although the AAII is a popular sentiment survey, it's not the only game in town. Another sentiment survey monitored closely by traders is Investors Intelligence, which you'll learn about next.

INVESTORS INTELLIGENCE

Name: Investors Intelligence Advisor Sentiment Survey

Where to find: www.schaefersresearch.com or www.market-harmonics.com

Note: You can also pay for a yearly subscription to Investors Intelligence at www.investorsintelligence.com.

Hint: You may also type the words **Investors Intelligence** in a search engine such as Google or Yahoo! to find the most recent survey results.

Time period: Weekly survey

The Lighter Side: Investors Intelligence, which I nicknamed "The Advisors," will keep you out of trouble when the markets get frothy or gloomy. Another little secret: Do the opposite of the advisors.

WHAT THE ADVISOR SENTIMENT SURVEY DOES

This weekly sentiment survey, published by Chartcraft, polls independent newsletter writers for a view of what the market might do
over the next six months: bullish, bearish, or neutral. Chartcraft
exchanges information with a variety of services, and it also analyzes newsletters received on the Internet, in the mail, and by fax.

STEP-BY-STEP: HOW TO READ THE ADVISOR
SENTIMENT SURVEY IN FIVE MINUTES

1. Type **www.schaefersresearch.com** in your Web address line.
2. Click once on the "Quotes and Tools" tab.
3. Scroll down and to the left. Under "Market Tools," click
   on "Investors Intelligence."
4. The weekly survey results appear on the left.
5. The Investors Intelligence survey will look something like
   Figure 1.2.

FIGURE 1.2

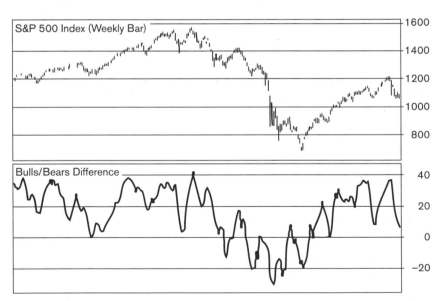

Source: Investors Intelligence

FIGURE 1.3

Bullish %	Bearish %	Correction %
38.50	31.90	29.60
39.80	28.40	31.80
39.30	29.20	31.50
43.80	24.70	31.50
47.20	24.70	28.10
56.00	18.70	25.30
54.00	18.00	28.00
53.30	17.40	29.30

Source: Investors Intelligence

6. Investors Intelligence also provides the results in a table like the one in Figure 1.3.

similar to AAII
do opposite

WHAT SIGNALS TO LOOK FOR

1. **Buy:** When independent financial newsletter writers are over 50 percent bearish, you may buy. At 60 percent, it's a screaming buy.
2. **Sell:** When independent financial newsletter writers are over 50 percent bullish, you may sell. At 60 percent, it's a screaming sell.
3. **Note:** These are not actionable trades, but only guidelines. Always use other indicators to confirm before buying or selling.

THE BACK STORY

A. W. Cohen, the founder of Chartcraft, Inc., decided to poll a group of experts in 1963 to find out what they thought of the stock market. The idea, of course, was to follow the experts' advice and make a killing on Wall Street.

After doing a number of surveys, Cohen discovered that the majority of newsletter writers were usually wrong at forecasting the market, especially at turning points. He learned that you could do well if you did the opposite of what the majority of the writers advised. Although officially called the Investors Intelligence Advisor Sentiment Survey, sometimes you might see it referred to as the bull/bear index. Their subscribers get the survey results immediately along with a daily e-mail.

HOW INVESTORS INTELLIGENCE WORKS

Chartcraft polls over 100 independent financial writers not affiliated with Wall Street about their views of the market. By polling independent writers who get paid to forecast market direction and advise their readers which way the market is headed, you'll get a range of viewpoints. (You might wonder why no one surveys professional advisors. The answer? More than likely, you'd get only one sentiment reading: buy.)

Just as with the AAII survey, the Advisor Sentiment Survey works remarkably well during market extremes, as long as you are contrarian.

It's actually intriguing because newsletter writers are supposed to be more sophisticated about the market. After all, they are getting paid to advise. And yet, just like the little guy, newsletter writers are often swayed by feelings of panic or euphoria.

In fact, many traders look at both the Advisor Sentiment Survey and the AAII survey to compare results. Often, sophisticated financial newsletter writers and individual investors share similar feelings about the market, especially when under stress.

Michael Burke, editor of Investors Intelligence, explains: "Many advisors are trend followers, but it is human nature for people and advisors to become more bullish when stocks are rising and more pessimistic when they are falling. Rising prices also seem to bring out more optimistic news and forecasts, while falling prices tend to do the opposite."

NOBODY'S PERFECT

Although the survey often gives early contrarian signals of market direction, which is useful information, it's not necessarily an actionable trade. Therefore, using sentiment indicators to precisely time the market is not always reliable. Generally, the survey results probably shouldn't be used by short-term traders to enter or exit the market. Many years ago, a study was conducted that claimed that the results of the Investors Intelligence survey as a contrarian indicator were not statistically significant. And yet, the survey still seems to work.

In addition, just like those on Wall Street, financial newsletter writers tend to be bullish, perhaps even more bullish than the individual investor. That might explain why sometimes the bullish sentiment of the Investors Intelligence survey tends to be a bit higher than for the AAII.

WHAT'S NEXT?

Now that you have an understanding of how to use sentiment surveys to monitor the crowd, we're going to do something different. To learn about the next indicator, you'll need a computer and the ability to bring up a stock chart. I'll take you through the process step-by-step.

The next set of indicators has been derived from the options market. If you are familiar with options vocabulary such as *calls*, *puts*, and *implied volatility*, you can skip the following sidebar. If you need a brief introduction to the options world, the information in the sidebar should help.

Options 101: Understanding Calls, Puts, and Implied Volatility

There are only two types of options, *calls* and *puts*. And with these two options, you can either buy or sell. Although there are dozens of sexy-sounding option strategies, all of the strategies are based on the buying and/or selling of calls and puts. For this book, we're interested in the buying of calls or puts.

When you buy a call, it is similar to going "long" a stock. It means you believe the underlying stock will rise in price. Retail investors who buy call options participate in the rising stock without having to actually buy the stock.

When you buy a put, it's similar to "shorting" a stock. It means you believe the underlying stock will fall in price. Retail investors who buy put options participate in the falling stock without actually having to short the stock. Sometimes people buy puts as insurance to protect their portfolios.

The next indicator, the Put/Call Ratio, is a way of monitoring whether more option traders are buying calls or buying puts. Keep in mind that institutions and hedge funds also buy calls and puts; they do so for entirely different reasons than retail options traders.

Retail options traders usually buy calls or puts based on an opinion: They buy calls if they think the market is going up, and they buy puts if they think the market is going down. Institutions often buy calls and puts to "hedge" their positions, and perhaps they have no opinion about the market. *Hint:* Pay attention to the retail options buyer.

Before you go on, I'd also like to introduce you to another vocabulary term from the options world: *implied volatility*. Implied volatility can be confusing for some people because it's difficult to define.

In simple terms, implied volatility represents a feeling of urgency that traders have about certain options. That urgency to buy pushes prices, and implied volatility, higher. More exciting stocks have higher implied volatility, and you must pay more to buy their options. Less exciting stocks have a lower implied volatility, so you can own them for less.

How does knowing about implied volatility help you? On the days when the stock market is volatile, especially when the direction is down, implied volatility can skyrocket. On these volatile days, not only do the option prices tend to go higher but also emotions may cause prices to soar.

And this is the key point: During the time when emotions in the options world and on Wall Street are at an all-time high, either positive or negative, you can turn to indicators for clues as to what might happen next. Panic and fear do not continue forever, nor do elation and overconfidence.

Now that you have a basic understanding of options vocabulary, it's time to take a look at the next indicator, the famous Put/Call Ratio.

CHICAGO BOARD OPTIONS EXCHANGE PUT/CALL RATIO

Name: CBOE Put/Call Ratio

Symbol: $CPCE (for "equity only") if using www.stockcharts.com*

Where to find: www.cboe.com and many other financial Web sites

Time period: Daily and weekly volume

The Lighter Side: The Put/Call Ratio, which I nicknamed "The Speculators," tracks the buying and selling of options. Not surprisingly, you'll probably do well if you bet against them.

Beginning with this indicator, we're going to use charts. In fact, the most challenging part of writing this book was finding a chart program that everyone could use. After all, there are dozens of brokerage firms and hundreds of online chart programs. Fortunately, I found a free, easy-to-use Web site that is devoted to market indicators: www.stockcharts.com.

Obviously, if you use your brokerage firm's charts, continue to do so. But if you don't know where to begin, you can follow along with me, step-by-step, as I introduce you to various market indicators. (For your information, I'm not affiliated with StockCharts.com in any way and receive no compensation for recommending them. They just happen to be a good place to visit if you're getting started with market indicators.)

Note: All of the "step-by-step" instructions below are aimed at anyone not familiar with chart software. If you are an experienced trader or you use a different chart program, feel free to skip the step-by-step instructions.

WHAT THE CBOE PUT/CALL RATIO DOES

The Put/Call Ratio tracks the volume of put and call options that trade on the Chicago Board Options Exchange (CBOE). Specifically, the idea is that option put buyers, who are aggressively bearish, are frequently wrong. And option call buyers, who are aggressively

---

*If you're using StockCharts.com, enter a $ before the symbol. Other chart programs might use different symbols. Ask your brokerage firm for details.

bullish, will also be wrong. When the indicator hits bullish or bearish extremes, it might be a clue to do the opposite.

STEP-BY-STEP: HOW TO READ
THE PUT/CALL RATIO IN FIVE MINUTES

1. Type **www.stockcharts.com** in your Web address line (or
   open any chart program).
2. On the right side of the screen, enter the symbol **$CPCE**,
   and press "Go."
3. The CBOE equity Put/Call Ratio will appear on the screen.
   It will look something like Figure 1.4.
4. **Hint:** You might notice red and blue lines displayed on the
   screen. These are moving averages, which we'll discuss later.
5. **Note:** You can also go directly to the www.cboe.com Web
   site for the current Put/Call Ratio. Under the "Quotes and
   Data" tab, select "CBOE Daily Market Statistics." Scroll to
   the middle of the page for the equity Put/Call Ratio. It
   will look similar to the chart in Figure 1.5.

WHAT SIGNALS TO LOOK FOR

1. **Buy:** An equity Put/Call Ratio higher than 1.0 (more puts
   are being bought) is a buy signal. Higher than 1.20 is a
   screaming buy.

FIGURE 1.4

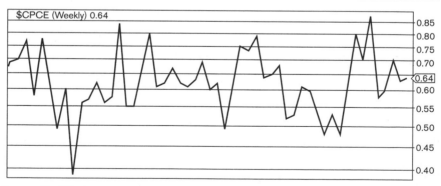

Source: StockCharts.com

FIGURE 1.5

Ratios	
Total Put/Call Ratio	1.19
Index Put/Call Ratio	1.64
Equity Put/Call Ratio	0.82
CBOE Volatility Index (VIX) Put/Call Ratio	0.25

Source: CBOE   *USE THIS*

2. **Sell:** An equity Put/Call Ratio lower than 0.75 (more calls are being bought) is a sell signal. Less than 0.50 is a screaming sell.

3. **Hint:** Look for a series of consecutive days of high or low Put/Call Ratios before taking action.

4. **Note:** The buy and sell ratios are not actionable trades, but only guidelines. Always use other indicators to confirm before buying or selling.

THE BACK STORY

Trader and author Martin Zweig has been credited with being the first to use the Put/Call Ratio to identify tops and bottoms by betting in the opposite direction. Zweig introduced the ratio in a series of articles after using it to make several accurate market forecasts. Although first launched in 1995, the CBOE added the equity Put/Call Ratio in 2003.

HOW THE CBOE PUT/CALL RATIO WORKS

The Put/Call Ratio is updated every 15 seconds by the CBOE. The purpose behind this contrarian indicator is that put and call buyers are generally wrong about the market, especially at tops and bottoms. Historically, retail speculators have a rather poor record of guessing market direction.

Although the Put/Call Ratio is constantly updated, it only flashes "actionable" signals a few times a year. Like other sentiment indicators, this ratio excels when the market is at one extreme or another. As speculators get more emotional, they'll buy loads of put options (because they think the market is going down) or loads of call options (because they think the market is going up).

By monitoring this crowd, you can get clues as when market tops or bottoms have been reached. When emotions are at a peak, more than likely the market is due for a reversal. This indicator has a pretty good record for calling tops and bottoms, but with some caveats.

NOBODY'S PERFECT

As with any sentiment indicator, the Put/Call data isn't perfect. When CBOE created the ratio, they placed all of the call and put options into one category (or "bucket," as it's known in the industry), which includes both professional and individual traders. They also have categories for index options as well as equity options. As a retail trader, it's recommended you only select the *equity* Put/Call Ratio, which is where you'll see the options trades of many market participants. (This means ignoring the index and total exchange categories.)

It gets a little confusing because on the CBOE the equity category also includes what is considered "nonoperating issues" such as exchange-traded funds (ETFs) and other securities that aren't common stocks. In other words, the CBOE equity Put/Call Ratio has been diluted with nonequity issues. You'll get a good feel for speculator sentiment if you use the equity-only portion, but keep in mind that these other securities may mislead you at times.

In the future, and this is a guess, it's possible that CBOE will rearrange the categories so they track only what individual speculators are buying and selling. When they make that change, the CBOE Put/Call Ratio will be even more valuable. But even with these minor complications, the Put/Call Ratio is a good contrarian indicator, which is why so many traders follow it.

Advanced Hints

Some traders apply a moving average to the Put/Call Ratio, for example, the 21-day exponential moving average (EMA), to smooth out fluctuations and look for additional buy signals. If you use the 21-day EMA, a ratio higher than 0.80 is a very strong buy, but as mentioned, over time ratio levels can change.

WHAT'S NEXT?

Many people don't realize there is another ratio calculated with options that also follows option participants. This is the new kid in town, the ISEE Call/Put Ratio, which I'd like to introduce next.

INTERNATIONAL SECURITIES EXCHANGE SENTIMENT INDEX CALL/PUT RATIO

Name: ISEE Call/Put Ratio

Where to find: www.ise.com/isee

Time period: Daily volume

The Lighter Side: The Call/Put Ratio, which I nicknamed "Speculators II," also tracks the buying and selling of options, but with whole numbers. Once again, you'll probably do well if you bet against the speculators, but you already knew that.

WHAT THE ISEE CALL/PUT RATIO DOES

The International Securities Exchange (ISE) Sentiment Index (ISEE) Call/Put Ratio tracks the call and put options of opening long transactions that trade on the International Securities Exchange. The ISEE Call/Put Ratio tends to be a contrarian indicator, which means when the indicator hits the bullish or bearish extremes, it's time to do the opposite.

HOW TO READ THE ISEE CALL/PUT RATIO IN FIVE MINUTES

1. Go to the ISE Web site (www.ise.com/isee).
2. Scroll to the middle of the page to "ISE Sentiment Index."
3. Three ISEE ratios will be displayed on your screen. It will look similar to Figure 1.6.
4. **Note:** Look at the "All Equities Only" columns. Focus on the ratio under the ISEE column. In the example above, it is 197. You can also look at the "All Securities" columns. In the example above, the ISEE ratio is 134.

(handwritten annotations: ↑ BUY   50 100   150 250 > NORMAL   ↓ SELL *)*

FIGURE 1.6

	All Securities				All Equities Only				All Indices and ETFs Only			
Time	Calls	Puts	Total	ISEE	Calls	Puts	Total	ISEE	Calls	Puts	Total	ISEE
16:10	350889	262747	613636	134	241971	122517	364488	197	108835	140182	249017	78
15:50	335032	253114	588146	132	230580	119274	349854	193	104369	133793	238162	78
15:30	322141	241792	563933	133	221702	112328	334030	197	100374	129418	229792	78
15:10	307513	231424	538937	133	208527	106497	315024	196	98928	124881	223809	79
14:50	297534	224968	522502	132	203767	103547	307314	197	93723	121375	215098	77
14:30	283760	217573	501333	130	195041	98895	293936	197	88676	118641	207317	75
14:10	269871	209264	479135	129	186356	94959	280715	197	83485	114872	198357	73
13:50	254382	202764	457092	125	173625	90740	264365	191	80673	111991	19264	72
13:30	230376	191405	421781	120	164573	85950	250523	191	65773	105432	171205	62
13:10	209917	182442	392359	115	148760	81669	230429	182	61132	100751	161883	61
12:50	199041	172854	371895	115	143400	74762	218168	192	55616	98070	153686	57
12:30	183283	162290	345573	113	133187	68960	202147	193	50071	93313	143384	54
12:10	174537	155608	330145	112	126796	66588	193384	190	47717	89013	136730	54

Source: Reprinted with permission from International Securities Exchange

5. **Hint:** You can also have ISE automatically send you a daily e-mail of the Call/Put results. Select the tab "How to Subscribe" in the middle of the page.

WHAT SIGNALS TO LOOK FOR

1. **Buy:** When the "All Equities Only" Call/Put Ratio is under 100 (more puts are being bought), it's a buy signal. Under 65 is a screaming buy.

2. **Sell:** When the "All Equities Only" Call/Put Ratio is over 250 (more calls are being bought), it's a sell signal. Over 350 is a screaming sell.

3. **Hint:** Look for a series of consecutive days of high or low call and put ratios before taking action.

4. **Note:** In the chart above, the ISEE ratios of 134 ("All Securities") and 197 ("All Equities Only") are well within the norm.

5. **Note:** These are not actionable trades, but only guidelines. Always use other indicators to confirm before buying or selling.

THE BACK STORY

ISE launched as the first all-electronic options exchange in the United States in 2000. It introduced its version of the sentiment indicator, the ISEE Call/Put Ratio, in 2002.

HOW THE ISEE CALL/PUT RATIO WORKS

Although many retail investors are not that familiar with ISE, with the benefit of hindsight, they were able to make two major adjustments to CBOE's version of the ratio. First, by dividing calls by puts (and multiplying by 100), the ISE ratio displays whole numbers rather than fractions. They believe whole numbers are easier for people to comprehend.

The ISE made a second adjustment: They removed market maker and firm trades from the Call/Put Ratio, which some feel is more representative of true investor sentiment. Keep in mind that when you look at the ISEE Call/Put Ratio, you are only looking at opening long trades of call buyers or put buyers.

Once again, because retail speculators generally have a poor record of calling tops and bottoms, the idea is to do the opposite. This ratio sometimes flashes a few reliable signals a year, and shines at market extremes. You want to look at a "cluster" of either high numbers or low ones for a possible signal. One extreme number is not significant, but a series of high numbers or low numbers could be a clue.

The Call/Put Ratio also has a good record of calling tops and bottoms, but since it has a relatively short record, you'll probably want to use both the CBOE and ISEE Put/Call indicators.

You probably know by now, but speculators tend to be swayed by emotion, so the rates at which they are buying call and put options give you insights into their thinking. Extreme readings, either high or low, tend to coincide with the changes in market direction. The idea is to be contrarian.

Perhaps the only complaint is that the indicator tends to be early. Because option speculators make split-second decisions under duress, more than likely they've made the wrong decision. However, applying a moving average can smooth out the choppiness. (You will learn about moving averages in Chapter 3.)

Advanced Hints

Sometimes it's best to look at a range of numbers. For example, the all-securities Call/Put Ratio may have the following range: bullish at 50 to 90; bearish over 150. Also, the equities-only Call/Put Ratio may have the following range: bullish at 65 to 130; bearish over 250.

Watch for extreme bullish/bearish readings that represent the 10 percent highest and lowest ISEE values over a period of time. Keep in mind that the bullish/bearish ranges should be periodically updated to reflect changes in market conditions and ISEE values.

WHAT'S NEXT?

By now you realize that the options market gives some very good clues as to investment sentiment. Next, I'd like to introduce you to another indicator that comes from the options world. More than likely, you've heard its name on television or read about it in a newspaper. The next indicator we'll learn about is the well-known and popular VIX.

CHICAGO BOARD OPTIONS EXCHANGE VOLATILITY INDEX

Name: Chicago Board Options Exchange Volatility Index (VIX)

Symbol: $VIX on www.stockcharts.com*

Where to find: www.stockcharts.com, any chart program, on the CBOE Web site, or reported daily in most major financial newspapers

Time period: Any

The Lighter Side: The VIX, which I nicknamed "Scaredy Cat," explodes higher when there is uncertainty and panic, and sinks when it's calm. Others have referred to it as the "Chicken Little Index" because it works best when people think the sky is falling.

---

*If you're using StockCharts.com, you enter a $ before the symbol, but this could vary with other chart programs. Ask your brokerage firm for the symbol it uses.

WHAT THE VIX DOES

The VIX indicator measures volatility and fear in the market by tracking the implied volatility of call and put options for a 30-day period.

STEP-BY-STEP: HOW TO READ
THE VIX IN FIVE MINUTES

1. Type **www.stockcharts.com** in your Web address line (or open any chart program).
2. On the right side of the screen under "Symbol," type **$VIX** and press Go.
3. **Hint:** To make the chart easier to read, change it to a line chart. The settings are below the chart. (In StockCharts.com, go to "Chart Attributes," and under "Type," there is a drop-down menu. Click and change to "Thin Line." Click on "Update" to accept the changes.)
4. **Note:** You can also change the time period of the chart to three months. (Under "Range," there is a drop-down menu. Change the default to "Three Months," and press "Update.")
5. It should look something like Figure 1.7.

FIGURE 1.7

Source: StockCharts.com

F I G U R E   1.8

VIX–CBOE Volatility Index

Open	High	Low	Close
22.64	22.87	21.76	21.99

Source: CBOE

6. **Note:** You can also go directly to the www.cboe.com Web site for the current VIX. Under the "Quotes and Data" tab, select "CBOE Daily Market Statistics." Scroll to the middle of the page. It will look similar to Figure 1.8.

WHAT SIGNALS TO LOOK FOR

1. **Buy:** When the VIX hits 40, there is panic in the options world, so you can consider buying stocks. If it goes over 50, the S&P 500 could be near a bottom.

2. **Sell:** When the VIX goes under 20, option traders are relatively calm. If the VIX goes below 12, option traders are too bullish, so you can consider selling stocks. The S&P 500 could be near a top.

3. **Hint:** 98 percent of the time, the VIX falls between 10 and 45, and when it is outside of this range, it is almost always on the high side.

4. **Note:** These are not actionable trades, but only guidelines. Always use other indicators to confirm before buying or selling.

THE BACK STORY

Launched in 1993 by the CBOE, the purpose of the VIX was to measure volatility for the S&P 500 stock index. The idea was intriguing: When stocks go down, option volatility (the VIX) goes up as more option traders buy puts to protect their stock portfolios, as an alternative to shorting, or to speculate. The VIX captured the imagination of the public because it was such an easy indicator to follow. Many believe it has the power to predict the market's future, and since its launch, it has had good buy signals, but the old saying "Look to buy when the VIX is high" is not a slam dunk.

HOW THE VIX WORKS

Technically, the VIX tracks the *implied volatility* of options in the S&P 500. As mentioned previously, implied volatility can be a confusing concept to some people. For our purposes, tracking the VIX gives you useful insights into what options traders think will happen.

Usually, a huge spike in the VIX will alert you to a short-term bottom or oversold condition. Many traders find it useful to put the VIX on a chart and compare it to how the market reacted in the past. With one glance at a chart, you can see extreme spikes. Remember, the higher the VIX goes, the more fear there is in the options market.

As with other sentiment indicators, the VIX works as a contrarian indicator. Therefore, as the VIX shoots higher because panicked option traders buy more puts for protection, you ought to consider doing the opposite (that is, you ought to consider buying stocks or call options).

NOBODY'S PERFECT

Unfortunately, although the VIX can identify emotional extremes, it has not always been a great timing indicator. Although it can alert you that a reversal is possible, it won't tell you when. It is the kind of indicator that can be checked each week for clues, but don't expect it to reveal more than you already know. Nevertheless, it is extremely useful to short-term traders, who often plot it on a chart with moving averages to generate buy and sell signals.

Short-Term Trading Strategies

If you're a short-term trader, there are a number of signals you can look for in the VIX:

1. Plot the VIX on a chart with moving averages (e.g., 150-day moving average) as support and resistance.

2. Plot the 10-day moving average on a chart. If the VIX spikes approximately 20 percent over its 10-day moving average, this could be a buy signal. Conversely, if the VIX drops well below the 10-day moving average, this could be a sell signal.

3. If you are an options trader, you can use the VIX as a guide when to sell covered calls. When the VIX is low and the market is calm with a slight bullish bias, it could be a good time to sell covered calls.

4. Short sellers watch the VIX to monitor investor nervousness.

WHAT'S NEXT?

After reading about sentiment indicators, you may already be thinking differently about the market. I hope so, because that was one of the goals of this book. After all, many people are surprised that going against the crowd can be profitable.

Before you learn about the next set of indicators, I'd like to formally introduce you to my first guest, recognized economist and author Bernard Baumohl. Fortunately, he stopped by to explain how he uses a variety of economic indicators to make market forecasts. If you are a trader or investor, it's essential you monitor economic conditions, and Baumohl will show you how.

BERNARD BAUMOHL: USING ECONOMIC INDICATORS

Baumohl's Favorite Economic Indicators

1. Institute for Supply Management (ISM)
2. Employment numbers
3. Unemployment rate
4. Payroll surveys
5. Cass Freight Index
6. American Association of Railroads report

According to many traders and investors, economic indicators not only provide insights on the current state of the economy and where it's been but also offer valuable clues on where it's heading. That's why certain economic reports, once released to the public, often cause sudden and violent swings in values in stocks, bonds, and currencies. Therefore, informed traders and investors keep a particularly close eye on forward-looking economic reports.

Bernard Baumohl, chief global economist at the Economic Outlook Group, confirms how important it is to include economic indicators in your trading or investing toolbox.

"Economic indicators can foretell if we're stumbling into recession—or about to experience a vigorous growth," Baumohl says. "Knowing where the economy stands in the business cycle at any point in time is essential if one is to achieve a profitable return on an investment. . . . Not only do these indicators help you decide whether to invest but also what to invest in—cash, stocks, or bonds—and where—the U.S., Europe, Japan, or the emerging countries."

He distinguishes between short-term traders and long-term investors, but both groups will find valuable clues in the economic reports.

MARKET MOVING EVENTS

If you don't think that economic indicators move the markets, all you have to do is watch the futures market at 8:30 a.m. Eastern Time. "Look at how quickly the stock and bond markets react to the economic indicators," Baumohl points out. "Traders try to anticipate what the economic reports will say and compare that with the actual numbers once they are released. The key is how surprised traders, and the markets, will be once the indicators are put out. A lot of money can instantly be made or lost, depending on which side of the market traders placed their bet."

Baumohl says that a day or two before an important economic indicator is released, professional traders will often contact their economic departments for their forecasts, or they will look at the consensus surveys to see what other analysts are expecting. Then they place their trades accordingly.

WATCH THE BUSINESS CYCLE

Although there are hundreds of economic indicators released on a weekly, monthly, and quarterly basis, not all of them are useful.

"Following them all will simply earn you a migraine," says Baumohl. "You've got to do it smartly. If we're in a recession, you won't look at the CPI [Consumer Price Index] or inflation numbers because they are expected to fall since demand for goods and services tends to be much weaker. What you will look for during a recession are any signs of life among the interest-sensitive sectors of the economy. That's typically where the seeds of a recovery can be found."

For example, you will want to look at home and auto sales, he says, because interest rates fall in a recession. At some point, however, the low cost of credit will fuel borrowing and spending. "You want to see if consumers are starting to take advantage of lower financing costs during a recession and resume buying homes and cars. Housing and auto sales are two very critical numbers to monitor during the later stages of a recession," Baumohl says.

Among the economic indicators you want to pay attention to is the ISM (Institute for Supply Management) numbers. "They reflect new orders placed to manufacturers, which eventually leads to greater production," Baumohl explains. "For example, during a recession businesses are content to sell from their existing inventory until there is a noticeable pick-up in sales. Eventually, the combination of low inventories and a rebound in demand for their products will suddenly bring in a surge of new orders from wholesalers and retailers. When manufacturers see their stock rooms getting empty, they'll quickly accelerate orders and production."

These orders are reflected in the monthly ISM indicator, which includes many other subcomponents such as the order backlog. "The bigger the backlog," he notes, "the more positive it is for the economy. The ISM is such a valuable indicator because it is so timely. It's released just one business day after the month being reported, and this gives you an early glimpse into the economy."

ECONOMIC INDICATORS FOR TRADERS

From a trader's viewpoint, Baumohl says, the hottest indicator is the monthly employment numbers from the Bureau of Labor Statistics. "Without a doubt the employment numbers, the unemployment rate, and the payroll surveys shake up the financial markets when they are released. Both the ISM release and the job numbers contain some of the freshest data on economic activity. Traders eagerly await these reports."

One of the secrets to reading economic indicators, Baumohl says, is not focusing so much on the headline numbers but instead "digging a little deeper into the reports to find much more forward-looking statistics than what is reported by the press. Look, everyone takes note of the payroll numbers and the unemployment rate, but what is also buried in this 30-page report among the statistics are the average weekly number of hours people worked during the previous month, as well as average overtime hours."

He says the average weekly hours worked is important because the more hours spent at work, the more income Americans bring home, which will encourage them to spend more. It could also lead to more hiring.

"Another hot number is temporary employment," Baumohl adds. "No indicator is better at telling you when the economy pivots from recession to recovery than temporary employment. Both turn at about the same time."

OTHER ECONOMIC CLUES

Because he is an economist, Baumohl looks more closely at the economic reports than most people. "These are just a small sample of the golden nuggets of information that many people don't bother seeking out. And yet it is only when you go beyond the headline numbers and dig into these economic reports that you have a better chance at understanding what is really going on in the economy. They offer many clues about where the economy is headed, but you have to get your hands dirty and dig in if you want to be rewarded with above-average returns on investments."

Two obscure indicators by private industry groups that Baumohl follows are the monthly Cass Freight Index and the weekly series by the American Association of Railroads. The Cass Freight Index measures the volume of goods trucks carry on the highway. "The more cargo that's being carried on trucks around the country, the higher the index," he says.

Baumohl also looks closely at a weekly report published by the American Association of Railroads, which computes the loadings of cargo on rail cars. "It's a good sign," he says, "when the volume of car loadings increases. It's remarkable how valuable some of these less well-known indicators are as a forecasting tool. They empower the individual investor to make intelligent decisions on how to invest instead of relying excessively on brokers or TV pundits."

THE STOCK MARKET AS AN INDICATOR

Another indicator you can't ignore is the stock market. "The stock market is a reasonably good leading indicator in and of itself," Baumohl says. "It's pretty good at predicting when an economy is about to emerge from a recession—and when it's approaching a downturn. Typically, the stock market turns bullish about four months before a recession ends, and it has a fairly good track record of warning that a recession is imminent."

And yet, Baumohl admits, the stock market is not a perfect science. "It is driven by confidence, fear, and sometimes panic. You can have all of the economic indicators pointing to strong growth, and even spectacular profits, but five minutes later you'll get a news flash that one country is near default on its debt and could spread to other countries. No matter what the economic indicators say, you'll see a sharp drop in the market."

THE PROBLEM WITH ECONOMIC INDICATORS

One temptation some people have when looking at economic indicators is to pick and choose only the statistics that support their personal views. "You have to be intellectually honest with yourself, and that means letting the indicators tell you the story on what the economy is up to," Baumohl points out. "You can't impose your views on the indicators. You have to be flexible and formulate your view based on the data."

Unfortunately, Baumohl cautions, "many analysts justify their views by manipulating the numbers. Once the indicators come out, you can torture the statistics all you want to prove a point. Eventually they'll confess to anything."

That isn't the way you should approach economic statistics, Baumohl says. "Each of these indicators is trying to tell you a story of what's going on in the economy, and you have to seriously consider it. If it turns out your initial assumptions do not coincide with the statistics, then you have to reassess the situation. Otherwise, you are fooling yourself."

It's not that easy to correctly interpret economic indicators. "No single indicator should be viewed as a crystal ball of where things are going," Baumohl explains. "You really have to look at a variety of different indicators. The goal is to find a pattern that emerges. You want them to corroborate each other. When several indicators point in the same direction, you can say with increasing confidence where the economy is headed and how financial assets should best be allocated."

Although reading economic indicators is a very intuitive process, he says, eventually the indicators line up together. "The only time you will get a confusing mixture of both positive and negative signals is when the economy approaches an inflection point. An inflection point occurs either at the lowest point of the business cycle or the peak of the cycle."

When the economy is expanding, he notes, there's a preponderance of positive numbers. In the middle of a recession, there is a preponderance of negative numbers. "But when you get to the turning points, that's when you will often get a confusing mixture of both strong and weak economic signals."

Perhaps most important, you have to be nimble. "Let's face it," Baumohl says. "A lot of what is going on in the world is unpredictable. There are so many economic and noneconomic events taking place every day, week, and month around the world that you can't stick to any rigid rules or guidelines. That's why economic forecasters and investors have to be agile and use good judgment."

CONSUMER MOODS

There is one group of indicators, however, Baumohl has placed above all others in importance: the three that foreshadow consumer spending. He explains: "No measure is more important than jobs. If people have a sense of job security and feel upbeat about future income growth, they will likely spend more. Secondly, when household wealth increases—which occurs when the value of their assets rises more than their personal liabilities—people will feel more comfortable about shopping. And finally, if your take-home pay increases faster than inflation, you have greater purchasing power, and this will also encourage you to spend more. All of these indicators come out on a regular basis and should be closely followed."

PUTTING ALL THE PIECES TOGETHER

Baumohl believes it's not difficult to put the economic indicators together and come up with an understanding of where the economy is headed. "It takes a little time to learn how to interpret economic statistics, but you don't need a Ph.D. in economics or math to do so," he says. "What you need above all is good judgment. Economics is more about what people think and do."

Bernard Baumohl is chief global economist at the Economic Outlook Group. He began his career as an analyst with the Council on Foreign Relations, a think tank specializing in international affairs. Baumohl later served as an economist at European American Bank with responsibilities to monitor the global economy and develop forecasts. Baumohl was also an award-winning economics reporter with *Time* magazine, who covered the news from New York, Washington, London, and Jerusalem. Apart from his role as chief global economist, Baumohl also teaches at the New York Institute of Finance and is an economics commentator on Public Television's *Nightly Business Report*. Baumohl is the author of *The Secrets of Economic Indicators: Hidden Clues to Future Economic Trends and Investment Opportunities* (Wharton School Publishing, 2nd edition). The bestselling book is the winner of the Readers Preference Editor's Choice Award for Finance and has been translated into several languages.

WHAT'S NEXT?

If this is the first time you've learned about market indicators, you might be either overwhelmed or eager to continue. If overwhelmed, don't worry, because the more you learn about indicators, the easier it gets. For those eager to go on, I'll now introduce you to the set of market indicators that I call "By the Numbers."

CHAPTER 2

By the Numbers

The next set of market indicators is favored by those who like to count. These indicators monitor the market primarily by displaying a running tally, such as which stocks are advancing or declining, or which have reached new highs or new lows.

These indicators are deceptively easy to use. Although they give you absolute numbers, interpreting the numbers correctly can be a challenge.

And now, I'd like to introduce you to a favorite of many traders and investors: New High–New Low.

NEW HIGH-NEW LOW

Name: New High–New Low

Where to find: www.stockcharts.com, almost any chart program, and in most financial newspapers

Symbol: $USHL if using StockCharts.com* (NYSE and Nasdaq combined)

Note: You can also use $NYHL (for NYSE) or $NAHL (Nasdaq).

Time period: Variable

---

*If you're using StockCharts.com, you enter a $ before the symbol, but this could vary among different chart programs. Ask your brokerage firm for the symbol it uses.

The Lighter Side: New High–New Low, which I nicknamed "The Runners," measures stocks that are making new highs or new lows. The goal is to advance to the front so they can be added to the new high list. Those that fail to make it get sent to the new low list.

WHAT NEW HIGH–NEW LOW DOES ~~BREADTH~~

The New High–New Low indicator tracks stocks that are making new highs or new lows for a specified time period.

STEP-BY-STEP: HOW TO READ THE
NEW HIGH–NEW LOW INDICATOR IN FIVE MINUTES

1. Type **www.stockcharts.com** in your Web address line (or open any chart program).
2. On the right side of the screen under "Symbol," type **$USHL**, and press "Go."
3. When the chart appears, you should see the 52-week New High–New Low graph for the NYSE and Nasdaq.
4. The chart should look something like Figure 2.1.

FIGURE 2.1

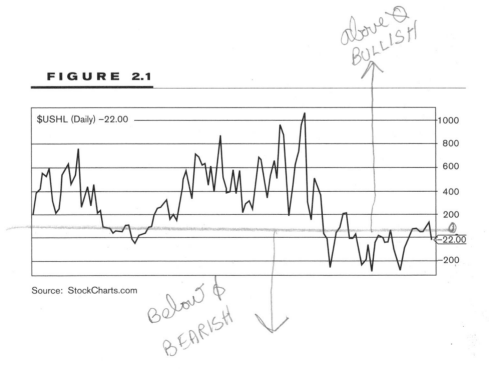

$USHL (Daily) –22.00

Source: StockCharts.com

WHAT SIGNALS TO LOOK FOR

1. **Bullish:** If the New High–New Low is positive (new highs surpass new lows), that indicates that market breadth is bullish.
2. **Bearish:** If the New High–New Low is negative (new lows surpass new highs), that indicates that market breadth is bearish.
3. **Note:** These are not actionable trades, but only guidelines. Always use other indicators to confirm before buying or selling.

THE BACK STORY

No one knows exactly who first started using the New High–New Low indicator. Author and trader Dr. Alexander Elder has been a huge fan of this indicator and highlighted it in his books. Those who use it claim the New High–New Low indicator is one of the most reliable indicators at monitoring the underlying *breadth* of the market (i.e., the number of stocks participating in the market's move).

HOW THE NEW HIGH–NEW LOW INDICATOR WORKS

The calculation for New High–New Low is straightforward. You subtract the number of new lows from the number of new highs. Really, that's it! Many financial newspapers publish a daily tally of new highs and new lows, but it can be more practical to see the results on a chart.

People will see if the *new high* list is expanding, which could indicate the market is rising and the market breadth is positive. Conversely, if the *new low* list is expanding, that could mean the market is falling and the market breadth is negative.

If you are monitoring the overall market, it's important to recognize whether the new highs, for example, are participating in a rising market. In particular, you want to spot signs of an important phenomenon, *divergence* (i.e., when the price goes in the direction opposite to that of the indicator).

For example, let's say the market is going higher but more and more stocks are suddenly falling off the new high list. In this case, because the market and the indicator are going in different directions, you have to question whether the market is as strong as it appears.

Keep in mind that in a bull market you may see an expansion of new highs, while in a bear market, more stocks might be making new lows.

OVERBOUGHT OR OVERSOLD

Another clue traders look for is whether the new highs and new lows have reached extreme levels. Of course it's positive if many stocks are making new highs. But if too many stocks are making new highs, that could also be a sign that the market is *overbought* (i.e., there is excessive buying).

If the market does get overbought, you could see more and more stocks dropping off the new high list. Stocks that were once in charge are suddenly losing their leadership. If too many stocks drop off the new high list, a change in the trend may be imminent.

And in a market that is *oversold* (i.e., there is excessive selling), eventually you may see more and more stocks dropping off the new low list. This often signals a short-term bottom.

It is also suggested that you look at the volume bars at the bottom of the chart to confirm whether the market is rising or falling on increased volume. Volume is discussed in more detail in Part Three, "Understanding Volume."

HOW TO USE NEW HIGH–NEW LOW

Chris Puplava, a registered investment advisor (RIA) at PFS Group, explains that as the market transitions from bearish to bullish, you see the percentage of stocks rising or falling. He explains the concept with a seasonal analogy: "As you go from summer to fall," he says, "you see the color of the leaves change, and some are falling. Just like the seasons, bull and bear markets don't change on a dime."

As you transition into a bear market, Puplava notes, "the percentage of stocks making new highs starts to fall. Fewer and fewer stocks are participating on the upside, and eventually the number of new stocks falling outweighs the number of stocks rising. On the other hand, at the end of a bear market, fewer and fewer stocks are participating on the downside."

What Puplava suggests is that traders and investors look for spikes on the chart rather than simply looking at absolute numbers. On the chart, he says, you can see what's happening as compared to the past. Doing so is more useful than just looking at a list.

NOBODY'S PERFECT

Although New High–New Low still remains one of the more popular indicators, it's not flawless. Some critics claim that although you can spot divergences using New High–New Low, the market may not react for weeks or months. In other words, perhaps the market rallies as fewer and fewer stocks make new highs, but the market doesn't lose steam as fast as some traders believe should happen.

Nevertheless, New High–New Low is extremely useful because it measures when traders are ready to take more risk. You can use this indicator to confirm the results of other indicators.

For Short-Term Traders

The basics of many trading systems say that stocks on the new high list tend to go higher while stocks on the new low list tend to go lower. Some traders apply a 10-day simple moving average to the chart to smooth out this indicator and identify buy or sell signals. Shorter time periods, from 3-day up to 20-day, are also popular with traders. Finally, some traders use this indicator to identify shifts in market psychology, especially when there is a sudden increase of new highs or new lows.

WHAT'S NEXT?

If you liked New High–New Low, you'll appreciate the next indicator, the Arms Index. It's relatively easy to read and follow, which is why it's been popular with traders, especially short-term traders. But as you'll find out, there are a few nuances to learn if you want to use it properly. And now, let's learn more about the Arms Index.

THE ARMS INDEX

Name: The Arms Index (TRIN)

Where to find: www.stockcharts.com, www.market-harmonics.com, or any stock chart*

Note: It's also displayed in tabular form in *Barron's*, the *Wall Street Journal*, and other financial papers.

Symbol: $TRIN if using StockCharts.com

Hint: Change the chart's "Type" default from "Candlesticks" to "Thin Line" for an easier read.[†]

Time period: Daily or weekly

The Lighter Side: This indicator, which I nicknamed "The General," is charging ahead fueled by rising stock prices and increasing volume.

WHAT THE ARMS INDEX DOES

This breadth indicator helps identify overbought and oversold conditions.

STEP-BY-STEP: HOW TO READ THE ARMS INDEX IN FIVE MINUTES

1. Type **www.stockcharts.com** in your Web address line (or open any chart program).
2. On the right side of the screen, type **$TRIN**. (Your chart might use a different symbol.)
3. When the chart appears, you should see the Arms Index on the screen.
4. The chart should look something like Figure 2.2.
5. **Hint:** To make the chart easier to read, change it to a line chart. (In StockCharts.com, go to "Chart Attributes," and

---

*If you're using StockCharts.com, you enter a $ before the symbol, but this could vary among different chart programs. Ask your brokerage firm for the symbol it uses.

[†]Later, I'll show you how to change the default chart settings on any chart. Once you learn how to do that, you can change time periods, line type, and most important, you'll find out where all of the other indicators are hidden!

FIGURE 2.2

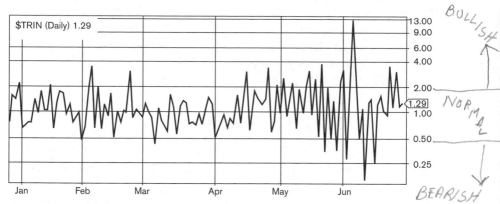

Source: StockCharts.com

under "Type," there is a drop-down menu. Click and change to "Thin Line." Click on "Update" to accept the changes.

6. **Note:** You can also change the time period to three months. (Under "Range," there is a drop-down menu. Change the default to "Three Months.")

WHAT SIGNALS TO LOOK FOR

1. **Buy:** If the Arms Index goes above 2.0 on the close, this could be a signal to buy. Above 4.0 (possible panic) could be a screaming buy.

2. **Sell:** If the Arms Index goes below 0.50 on the close, this could be a signal to sell. Below 0.30 (overexuberance) could be a screaming sell.

3. **Chart note:** The extreme reading of 13.22 on June 7 was very unusual, indicating short-term panic, and suggests, according to the Arms Index, an imminent rally (which actually occurred for the next two weeks).

4. **Note:** These are not actionable trades, but only guidelines. Always use other indicators to confirm before buying or selling.

THE BACK STORY

When Richard Arms created the Arms Index, he didn't have much time to think of a proper name. After all, its sudden popularity was a big surprise to him, especially when it showed up as an indicator on the New York Stock Exchange (NYSE), where it has remained for over 50 years.

HOW THE ARMS INDEX WORKS

The Arms Index (TRIN) calculates how much volume is associated with rising or declining stock prices on the NYSE or Nasdaq. Therefore, if NYSE stock prices are rising on increasing volume, that's bullish. And if the NYSE stock prices are falling on increasing volume, that's bearish.

The Arms Index was designed to be primarily a short-term trading tool, although people have used it to determine if the markets are overbought or oversold. When you read the index for the first time, you'll see it is displayed as a ratio. Therefore, the lower the ratio, the more bullish it is for the market. Conversely, the higher the ratio, the more bearish it is for the market.

WHEN TO BUY OR SELL

Tim Ord, author of the *Secret Science of Price and Volume* (Wiley, 2008), checks the Arms Index on a daily basis. "Although the Arms Index changes all day, it is most useful at the close," he says. "This is most revealing because traders are making their minds up at the close. It's mass psychology."

Therefore, he points out, if you're in a downtrend and the Arms Index closes above 3.0, it is a climatic panic and could mean that everyone is heading for the exits. At 3.0 he starts to get interested. When it gets as high as 5.0 or 6.0, then he knows that something major is happening. When the Arms Index reaches these extreme levels, it could lead to a climatic low.

The problem, he cautions, is that the Arms Index could stay in that position for a long time, even several months. "Once the Arms Index went to 6.0 and stayed there for a month," says Ord. "This was a major low."

Some short-term traders were impatient, wondering why the market didn't reverse immediately. But finally, after a month, the market turned around and went higher. "It took a while but the Arms was right," Ord notes.

The Arms Index also works in reverse. If the indicator gets below 0.30, which is another climatic reading, it means a lot of people are buying. That could lead to a climatic high.

NOBODY'S PERFECT

Like any indicator, the Arms Index is not perfect. Its signals seem to be most reliable at picking bottoms rather than tops. Also, some traders say that looking at the Arms Index with NYSE may not give you an accurate picture, so also look at the Arms Index using the Nasdaq Composite.

For Short-Term Traders

Many traders apply a simple moving average (the 10-day is common) to the Arms Index to smooth out the volatility and make it easier to read. You can also apply the 20- or 21-day moving average for intermediate trades and the 50-day for the long term.

When the Arms Index moves below 1.0, there is a strong likelihood of a short-term reversal, but use other indicators to help with timing.

WHAT'S NEXT?

As already mentioned, to really learn about market indicators it's extremely helpful to get inside the minds of their creators. Therefore, I'm pleased to introduce Richard Arms, creator of the Arms Index, who was kind enough to share a few of his thoughts about the indicator he created.

RICHARD ARMS: CREATOR, THE ARMS INDEX

Richard Arms, president of the Arms Advisory, created the Arms Index in 1967. "Back in the sixties when I dreamed of this index, I was working for a brokerage firm called E.F. Hutton, which most people don't remember," Arms says. "When we moved into our new offices, the brand-new machines displayed quotes on a small screen. I realized that in addition to getting advances and declines, I could also get the volume of the advancing stocks and the volume of the declining stocks."

That's when he thought of his indicator. "I came up with this stupidly simple indicator that combined the volume with the advancing and declining stocks," he explains. "I was the first guy to think of it, but if I hadn't, someone else would have. The very simplicity is what makes it so effective." Even today, many traders and investors use the Arms Index to measure the bullishness or bearishness of the entire market.

"I had no idea it would be this big," Arms says. "I sent it to our technical analyst, who sent it to Alan Abelson at *Barron's*. Abelson called me and said, "I want to publish this thing." Getting a call from Abelson, Arms recalls, was like getting a call from the president.

After Abelson published the ratio in *Barron's*, it took off. "Soon it was on quote machines all over Wall Street." Arms says he was the most surprised that his indicator became so popular. "I went to New York for an interview and the guy I met had my index on his computer."

When his indicator was first published in *Barron's*, it was called the Trader's Index. The Quotron machines on Wall Street needed a four-digit label, so they called it the TRIN. "If you go to the NYSE Big Board," Arms says, "it's still called the TRIN. I would love to have it changed."

INTERPRETING THE ARMS INDEX

The Arms Index works like this: After you calculate the number of advances and declines over advancing and declining value, the Arms Index displays a ratio: The lower the ratio, the more bullish the market.

When the index was created, the calculation remained as a ratio (without converting it to a whole number), so lower numbers are better. By then, it was too late to change the way the numbers were displayed. People still approach Arms asking why little numbers are good and big numbers are bad.

"I tell audiences if the low numbers bother you that much, then think of it as a golf score," he explains. "So 0.25 is a very bullish number. It means that the flow of money is going to the buy side of the market. These stocks are getting too much money. To interpret, we have underlying bullishness that can't move the market. You have to wonder what is going on, so you take a second look."

Arms says it's not too difficult to calculate his index. "Let's say we had 2,038 stocks up and 985 stocks down," he explains. "By dividing 2,038 by 985, you come up with a 2.07 ratio. It means twice as many stocks are up than down. Are the up stocks getting more or less shares?" NUMERATOR ADV/DECLIN # OF STKS (RATIO)

To find out, he will look at the volume for the day. "For example, let's say the up volume for this day was 855,952, and the down volume was 276,138," Arms says. "When you divide up and down volume, you get a ratio of 3.10. On this day, twice as many stocks were up as down. And the up stocks were getting three times as much volume as the down stocks. They were getting far more volume than they should." DENOMINATOR ADV VOL/DECLIN (RATIO) VOL

When we divide the 2.07 ratio by 3.10, we get an Arms Index of 0.67. "When you get a lot of low numbers for too long a time, then you have a market that has gone up too much," Arms points out.

Although Arms doesn't like to give hard numbers, he admits that anything above 1.25 is a clue that the market is oversold, while anything below 0.75 is a good buy point. "But that's very general because the whole spectrum tends to shift in a bull or bear market," he cautions.

Arms constantly tweaks his index, as do others who've created indicators. He'll take the day's ratio and plug it into the 10-day moving average. He also created a complicated indicator he calls the "Yo-Yo Index," which measures how much volume is needed to push the market to a specific price. Besides what he created, the only major indicator Arms looks at is MACD (Moving Average Convergence Divergence; see Chapter 3).

"I stick with mathematical indicators as much as I can because everything that can be known about the market is in its price and volume," says Arms. "Not just dividends, earnings, and management but even the little old lady who sold 100 shares to make a house payment. Everything is in there."

RATIO OF ADV/DECLIN # OT STKS

RATIO OF ADV VOL/DECL VOL   LOW-BULL
                                 HIGH-BEAR

ADVICE ON USING INDICATORS

When using the Arms Index or any other indicator, Arms recommends keeping it simple. "Some people make things a lot more difficult than they need to be," he notes. Perhaps most important, you need to think what the indicators are telling you. Although everyone is looking at the same data, correctly interpreting the information is essential. And this means really thinking and analyzing.

"An indicator is only as good as the person interpreting it," Arms says. "People want me to give them hard numbers—'If it's 1.25, do you buy, or don't you?'" He says that over time you develop a feel for the numbers.

A VOICE IN THE WILDERNESS

Arms mentions, "I've been in this business for half a century. I find that when I am most right is when I am most alone, like a voice crying in the wilderness. For example, when I tell everyone we've reached a market top, they are crying, 'Noooo!'"

For Arms, when too many people deny there is a market top, it's a clue the market has reached a top.

Richard Arms has spent nearly half a century following, trading, and writing about the market. Best known for his Arms Index, or TRIN, his other major contributions to Wall Street methodology include Equivolume Charting, Ease of Movement, Volume Adjusted Moving Averages, Volume Cyclicality, and a number of volume-based indicators. These tools are revealed and explained in his six books, the most recent titled *Stop and Make Money*. Arms has received many of the highest awards in technical analysis, including the Market Technicians Association award for lifetime achievement. He has been inducted into the Traders Hall of Fame. Located in Albuquerque, New Mexico, Arms publishes the *Arms Advisory* and advises a select group of institutions. He also writes a twice-weekly column for RealMoney, a subsection of TheStreet.com.

WHAT'S NEXT?

As you continue learning about indicators, keep in mind that you aren't going to like all indicators. One of the purposes of this book is to introduce you to the main indicators so you can pick and choose the ones that are the most useful to you.

The next indicator, the Advance-Decline Line, is another favorite of traders and investors. At the market close, you may hear TV commentators say something like, "In today's market action, advancing stocks outnumbered declining stocks on the New York Stock Exchange by a ratio of 2 to 1."

But as you'll see, the final tally can be read or, perhaps even better, plotted on a chart.

ADVANCE-DECLINE LINE

Name: Advance-Decline Line

STOCKCHARTS.COM

Symbol: $NYAD on StockCharts.com*

Where to find: The Advance-Decline Line is included in many chart programs. You can also look up the precise number of advances and declines for most market indexes in many financial newspapers. *Note:* Data vendors use different calculations for determining advances and declines so results may vary.

Time period: Based upon daily action

The Lighter Side: The Advance-Decline Line, which I nicknamed "The Leaders," is a running cumulative total of advancing and declining stocks. After you determine who's ahead, the next move is yours.

WHAT THE ADVANCE-DECLINE LINE DOES

This simple indicator plots a running cumulative total of advancing stocks minus the declining stocks each day. It helps traders measure how many stocks are taking part in a rising or falling market.

STEP-BY-STEP: HOW TO READ THE
ADVANCE-DECLINE LINE IN FIVE MINUTES

1. Type **www.stockcharts.com** on your Web address line (or open any chart program).

*If you're using StockCharts.com, enter a $ before the symbol. Other chart programs might use a different symbol for this indicator. Ask your brokerage firm for details.

2. On the right side of the screen, type **$NYAD**, which is a chart of the net advances (i.e., advances less declines) on the New York Stock Exchange.

3. When the chart appears, at first the Advance-Decline Line may resemble a seismograph. Scroll below the chart to "Type" under "Chart Attributes." In the drop-down menu, change the line type from "Candlesticks" to "Cumulative." Press "Update."

4. The Advance-Decline Line will appear as a smooth line— in fact, something like what is shown in Figure 2.3.

WHAT SIGNALS TO LOOK FOR

1. **Bullish:** The line is rising, which means advancing stocks outnumber declining stocks.

2. **Bearish:** The line is falling, which means declining stocks outnumber advancing stocks.

3. **Note:** These are not actionable trades, but only guidelines. Always use other indicators to confirm before buying or selling.

4. **Advanced chart hint:** Overlay a chart of the New York Composite ($NYA). Compare the direction of the

FIGURE 2.3

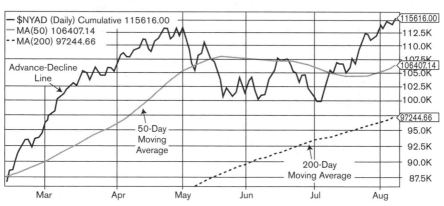

Source: StockCharts.com

Advance-Decline Line with the New York Composite, which is where this indicator comes from.

THE BACK STORY

The Advance-Decline Line is one of the earliest and most watched daily indicators to determine market breadth, that is, whether the rally is widespread and broad. You have a choice: calculate the advances and declines yourself or see it visually on a chart.

HOW THE ADVANCE-DECLINE LINE WORKS

The number of advances and declines are usually announced at the end of each trading day. For the Advance-Decline Line to be really useful, however, you have to do some detective work. Just knowing the absolute numbers isn't good enough. Some traders will confirm the advancing over declining issues by using volume. For example, stocks are advancing on higher volume, that can mean it's a stronger move.

Although the advances and declines can be calculated without a chart, it's much easier to see it visually. With one glance, you can observe the direction of the Advance-Decline Line. If the Advance-Decline Line is rising, more stocks are advancing than declining. If the Advance-Decline Line is falling, more stocks are declining than advancing. Some traders want to see if the Advance-Decline Line "diverges" from the market price.

For example, if the market is rising but the Advance-Decline Line is falling (*divergence*), that could be significant. It could mean the number of advancing stocks is falling off, and it may mean the rising market is weak. Traders may consider this a warning that the uptrend may be coming to an end. It's considered much stronger, and healthier, when the Advance-Decline Line and market are trending in the same direction.

NOBODY'S PERFECT

One of the problems with the Advance-Decline Line is how it's calculated. If a stock goes up a penny, it's considered an advance. And if a stock goes up by $5, it's an advance. So unless you look deeper, you don't know what is really going on.

Another problem with the Advance-Decline Line is that the signals are sometimes slow, especially with divergences, so you won't get a meaningful signal for weeks or even months. If you do use the Advance-Decline Line, it gives you a general idea which stocks are leading the market, but it probably isn't the best timing indicator. In fact, some traders suggest not using it for timing at all.

If you use the NYSE Advance-Decline Line, you should be aware that the advances and declines include all issues, including many "nonoperating securities" (e.g., closed-end bond funds). On the NYSE, all issues are treated equally, so some of these nonoperating securities can cause some people to misinterpret the results. Once again, you have to look more closely to see which stocks are leading the market.

To solve this limitation, some traders also look at the Nasdaq Composite Index or S&P 500 Advance-Decline Line. These have many common stocks in them, but there are limitations with them as well. Nasdaq has somewhat looser requirements than the NYSE, which tends to give the Nasdaq Advance-Decline Line a downward bias.

One idea is to study the nonoperating issues and common stocks separately. The nonoperating issues, which can be used to monitor liquidity, are like "canaries in a coalmine," as one pro put it. When liquidity is good, these issues will do well, and when liquidity is scarce, the nonoperating issues do poorly, which can adversely affect the stock market.

This analysis is not meant to confuse you but only to let you know how each indicator has nuances. The lesson is that if you use indicators, you must really learn everything about them. Each has its advantages and disadvantages. Using an indicator without being aware of its limitations is like driving a car with one hand behind your back.

For Short-Term Traders

On the S&P 500 Advance-Decline Line, each component has an equal weight of 1/500. This means that the Advance-Decline Line calculation looks more at smaller size stocks than larger size ones. In other words, when the Advance-Decline Line increases to a higher low, while the S&P 500 makes a new low, it means that money is probably moving from large caps into small caps, which indicates that risk taking is back in the markets, and the markets could move higher.

Conversely, if the Advance-Decline Line makes a lower high while the S&P 500 makes a new high, it means that money is probably going into large caps, which is a sign of unwillingness to take new risk. The market might pull back down.

Finally, a number of traders have turned to short-term trading tools such as the NYSE McClellan Oscillator, briefly explained in Chapter 12, for more reliable signals. Traders usually use this momentum oscillator with the McClellan Summation Index. For a daily list of advances and declines, as well as charts of the McClellan Oscillator and Summation Index, go to www.mcoscillator.com, and select "Market Breadth" from the main menu.

Tom McClellan, owner of the above Web site, is the son of Sherman and Marian McClellan. His parents originally developed the McClellan Oscillator and the Summation Index in 1969, based on the work of P. N. Haurlan, a real rocket scientist. McClellan continued the work his parents started. He explains that "the McClellan Oscillator is not going to tell you something different from the Advance-Decline Line. But it will give you more in-depth information so you'll know the complete story."

Unfortunately, he says, not everyone fully understands how to use the oscillator. "If all you do is look at the numerical value of the McClellan Oscillator," McClellan says, "you're ignoring 99 percent of the most useful information. If all you know is the number, you don't know what the trend is. It's like forecasting the weather by only knowing the current temperature. That would be a very limited way of forecasting. Therefore, you can only use the McClellan Oscillator if you understand its value relative to yesterday or last week." The key to understanding it, he says, is looking at it on a chart.

Although the McClellan Oscillator can take some time to learn, it enhances the information received from the Advance-Decline Line. Basically, when the 19-day exponential moving average (EMA) is below the 39-day EMA, the McClellan Oscillator will generate a negative value. It means that declining issues are stronger than advancing issues. Conversely, if the 19-day EMA is above the 39-day EMA, the McClellan Oscillator will generate a positive value. It means that advancing issues are stronger than declining issues.

WHAT'S NEXT?

As we continue on, you might be making a list of your favorite indicators. Over time, you'll take the indicators you like best and practice with them in real life.

And now, I'd like to introduce my next guest, well-known trader, bestselling author, and creator of numerous indicators, Larry Williams. I'm sure you'll enjoy reading about two of his passions: trading and creating more indicators.

LARRY WILLIAMS: CREATOR, WILLIAMS %R AND ULTIMATE OSCILLATOR

Larry Williams, a prolific author and trader, is best known in the trading community for creating two well-known market indicators, Williams %R and the Ultimate Oscillator. (*Note:* A chart of Williams %R is located in Chapter 12.)

It was back in the 1960s when he created his first indicator. "There weren't very many indicators then," Williams recalls. "So I looked at other indicators and wondered if there was another way of skinning that cat. I had ideas and insights about the market and wondered how I could express those things. When you stay up late and drink some wine, it's amazing what your mind comes up with."

There were few traders in those days, he remembers. "There wasn't a CNBC, and we got the *Wall Street Journal* a few days late. But people wondered why I was living in a nice house and driving a nice car. I wrote a newsletter and lectured. I never expected to end up in life where I am now."

He attributes his ability to create indicators to seeing the world differently than other people. "I started as an art major in college, so I'm a very visual person. Because of my art background I've been trained to look and see patterns. While the average person might see a graph, I see colors and shades and bugs crawling around. It's not that I'm gifted; I was fortunate enough to be trained."

He remembers asking a friend about a list he saw of the most active stocks in the newspaper. "'What does this mean?' I asked my friend. He told me that if you bought a stock yesterday, today you would have made $100. Back in 1962, $100 was like a thousand dollars today. So I told him, 'You mean if I do this I don't have to go to work? That's for me!' It looked so easy. Well, I've been working hard at it ever since."

Although Williams creates mathematical indicators, he insists he's not a mathematician. He notes that "I'm primarily a trader who is attracted to that $1 to $2 a day. People have probably written more about my indicators than I ever did." The reason he created his indicators was to help determine when the market was overbought or oversold on a short-term basis. "I was just trying to survive," he remembers.

UNDERSTANDING CROWD BEHAVIOR

Although the goal of many indicators is to predict future market behavior, Williams is cautious. "Predicting is a tough business," he says, while admitting he's created a few indicators with predictive power.

"I also do a lot of forecasting work based on market cycles," he says. "There are harmonics of price that do tend to carry into the future." An oversimplification, he says, would be to study 10- to 13-year cycles within longer-term 100-year cycles. "It's been pretty accurate," he notes, calling it a road map of what should take place in the future.

Because Williams sees things visually, he trades based on what's in front of him. "Actually, there are 28 relationships between yesterday's closing price and today's closing price," he says. "Most people haven't taken the time to figure those out, let alone see them."

Although Williams is known for his technical indicators, he also believes fundamentals are important. "Charts don't move the markets," he points out. Remembering a logic class he took in college, "A can't predict A." Therefore, Williams says it is illogical to assume that price can predict price. It's important, therefore, to understand the bigger picture.

What Williams did learn about indicators is that they ultimately measure human emotion. "It's like what Pavlov did with the salivating dogs," he says. "If markets move up so much, there's a point where the human mind says, 'Aha! I want to buy that.' That's the nature of how humans are wired."

He explains that many indicators show you what the crowd and the trend are doing. "The indicators are a symptom that gives you a clearer view of what's going on now. I don't know if the technical indicators are that predictive, but they show you where you are. If you look at price itself, that's as deceptive as a Hollywood starlet. You don't know what the hell is going on. So we need indicators to give us a better view of whether this is a Hollywood starlet or a real queen."

E = MC²: THE EMOTIONAL
CHALLENGES OF A TRADER

Williams admits that the life of a trader can be difficult. "There are always crossed emotions," he says. "I might have a $50,000 profit in bonds right now, but a couple of days ago it was $65,000. Should I have gotten out earlier? Is my stop too close or too far away? Every day you have emotional banter in your mind. It's always there; it's the nature of this business. Every business has it, but it's more immediate in trading because it's right in front of you. Every tick lets you know whether you are losing or winning."

After 50 years of trading, Williams has learned to trust his emotions. "Now my emotions are a bit like an old bottle of wine that has matured," he says. "They might not be as clear and sharp as they once were, but our emotions are built on our experience, and my experience is far different from someone who has been trading for 5, 10, or 15 years."

When he started out, he said he'd be better off doing the opposite of what his emotions were. "When you're young and growing up as a cowboy in Montana riding rodeo and playing football, I'd push all the chips forward. It was very macho. That's great when you're right, like the time I turned $10,000 into $1 million at a real-time trading championship."

Now, he says, his position size is less aggressive but he sleeps a lot better. "And I don't have margin calls anymore," he quips, only half-jokingly.

Williams learned a lot of lessons about the market by observing what happens in Las Vegas. "The whole adage in Vegas is that to win big, you have to bet big," he says. "They tell you that to separate you from your money."

Therefore, if you bet big in the stock market, "that losing trade is going to come and you will lose your house. If you bet big, you will blow up at some point. So you never bet big." To win big in the stock market, he says, you have to bet small. "I always bet small."

Even if everything lines up and Williams sees a perfect chart pattern, he won't bet beyond his traditional trade size. "I can be wrong," he explains. "I can be wrong three or four times in a row."

In fact, he says that accepting losses is one of the key attributes of a successful trader. "When you trade, you know you are going to be wrong. People who can't accept being wrong are going to blow up their accounts. If you trade often enough, you will have a losing trade. When it comes to trading, you'd better be able to say, 'Oh no, bad trade. Let's find another one.'" That is another reason why he never makes a trade that goes beyond his comfort zone.

Williams summarizes how he manages risk by using Einstein's famous equation, $E = MC^2$. "Einstein had to be a commodity trader," he quips, "because that's a commodity equation. E = emotion. M = money. C = the number of contracts you have squared. So your emotions are equal to the amount of money you have and the contracts you spread them out on."

He explains that some people can withstand a 20 percent loss and be emotionally fine, while others can't. "You have to find your emotional quotient. At what point can you go to sleep with that percentage of your account at risk? Some people can't handle it. So you'd better find what works for you so you don't become irrational and do the wrong things because of your emotions."

THE PROBLEMS WITH INDICATORS

Although Williams has worked with indicators most of his life, he is painfully aware of their limitations. "Many indicators are giving the same message because they are massaging the same numbers," he says. "There isn't that much difference between the RSI and Stochastics and Williams %R."

Another problem with many indicators, Williams says, is they work off one time frame. Williams created the Ultimate Oscillator, which is included in numerous chart programs, to solve this problem. "What I did was combine three different time periods, the 7-day, 14-day, and 28-day, all into one index." The Ultimate Oscillator works well during volatile markets, such as when the market is overbought short term but not overbought long term.

One goal, Williams believes, is to understand how the indicators you use fit into the bigger picture. "The market is erratic and irrational," he notes. "There are a lot of black swans flying around every day. When I first started trading in the sixties, I read the books. And I lost a lot of money because the books were wrong. The indicators didn't work the way the author said they did. That was a big surprise. As Ronald Reagan used to say, 'Trust, but verify.'"

Perhaps most important, Williams says, is learning how to read the indicators you do use. "I see a lot of new traders looking at so many indicators on their charts they don't do anything. You have to be careful of that. I also see a lot of people toss a bunch of indicators into a Cuisinart, which they call their computer, and out comes this gobbledygook blend of something no one recognizes."

Williams constantly thinks of creating new indicators. His latest creation, Indicator Analyst, is a bit different, however. It is designed to backtest the predictive power of other indicator patterns.

"It analyzes your indicator and lets you know if it's any good," Williams says. "And you know what's really interesting? Usually indicator patterns don't predict a damn thing!" Even the indicators that had repeatable patterns were inconsistent.

For Williams, who rarely gives up, this means going back to his indicator board and creating a new indicator, perhaps one that successfully forecasts the market's future.

Larry Williams began following the markets in 1962 and was a full-time trader by 1967. He went on to write nine bestselling books on futures in stock trading. As one of the Robbins World Cup trading champions, Williams was the highest return ever posted. The indicators he has created are used throughout the world, including his Williams %R, the Ultimate Oscillator, Accumulation Distribution, and the VIX Fix. Williams no longer publishes a newsletter but spends most of his time as an active trader with some limited teaching to individual students. His Web site is www.Ireallytrade.com.

WHAT'S NEXT?

For many of you, the next section could be one of the most important. After all, when people talk about market indicators, they often mean technical market indicators such as the ones you'll learn about next.

If you've never used technical indicators before, don't worry. They're not that difficult to learn, as long as you take it step-by-step. I'll do my best to keep it that way, but I also throw in a few surprises for experienced traders. And now, let's get technical.

CHAPTER 3

Let's Get Technical

If you have heard that technical indicators are too complicated, relax. Although some indicators look like seismographs when plotted on a chart, I'll do my best to make them understandable. The great thing about using technical indicators is they can be as simple or as complicated as you want to make them.

Keep in mind that traders put market indicators on a chart for one main reason: it creates a powerful visual. One look at a chart (a picture is worth a 1,000 words) and you can see where the market is headed. Although not everyone believes in using technical indicators, they are extremely useful tools whose signals shouldn't be ignored. I have found it quite interesting how many professional investors, as well as traders, rely on technical indicators to make trading decisions.

Important note: All of the technical indicators described in this section can also be used on individual stocks. Rather than typing the symbol for a market index, type in a symbol for the individual stock.

WHO ARE YOU GOING TO CALL? THE HELP DESK

Although I will make this section as clear as possible, if you get confused along the way, you should call the Help Desk at your brokerage firm. As long as you are a customer, there should be a team of specialists trained to answer questions about any of the market indicators included in this book. More often than not, you won't go wrong talking to professionals who work at the Help Desk.

LET'S GET STARTED

Although many of the indicators you'll learn about are based on complicated mathematical formulas, our main focus is on using indicators to get into or out of the market. And now, I'd like to introduce one of the most popular market indicators: Moving Averages.

MOVING AVERAGES

Name: Moving Averages

Where to find: www.stockcharts.com or any chart program

Default settings: 50-day and 200-day

Time period: Weekly for longer-term signals; daily for shorter-term signals

Favorite market: Trending

The Lighter Side: Moving Averages, which I nicknamed "Your Best Friend," are designed to keep you on the right side of the trend and out of trouble, just like a good friend should.

WHAT MOVING AVERAGES DO

The Moving Averages indicator helps determine if a trend has ended or begun.

STEP-BY-STEP: HOW TO READ
MOVING AVERAGES IN FIVE MINUTES

1. Type **www.stockcharts.com** in your Web address line (or open any chart program).

2. On the right side of the screen, type **$SPX**, a symbol for the S&P 500 Index. *Note:* If you want, you can also choose $INDU (Dow Jones Industrial Average) or $COMPQ (Nasdaq Composite).

3. When the chart appears, you should see the 50-day and 200-day simple moving averages on the screen along with the market index, $SPX.

FIGURE 3.1

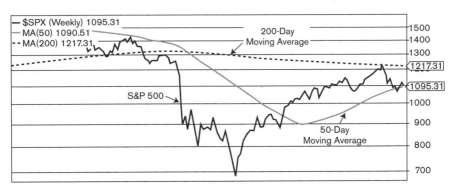

Source: StockCharts.com

4. On your computer screen, the 50-day line is blue, and the 200-day line is red.
5. The chart should look something like Figure 3.1.

WHAT SIGNALS TO LOOK FOR

1. **Buy:** If the index or stock crosses above the 50-day or 200-day moving average, that could be a signal to buy.
2. **Sell:** If the index or stock crosses below the 50-day or 200-day moving average, that could be a signal to sell.
3. **Note:** These are not actionable trades, but only guidelines. Always use other indicators to confirm before buying or selling.
4. **Hint:** This is almost the same chart you saw at the beginning of Part One, but now we have added moving averages. Notice how adding moving averages helps give you clues about the current trend. In the chart above, the S&P 500 is in very dangerous territory. Will it drop below the 50-day moving average?

THE BACK STORY

Richard Donchian is credited with being the first to develop moving averages while working at various investment firms.

Reportedly, Donchian's fascination with the stock market grew after he read a book about renowned stock trader Jesse Livermore.

After initially losing money in the 1929 crash, Donchian developed a technical trading system called "trend following" using the moving averages of commodity prices. Trend following was the basis of the Turtle Trading System, popularized by trading wizards William Eckhardt and Richard Dennis.

Another early pioneer of moving averages was J. M. Hurst, who developed a moving average system outlined in his challenging book *The Profit Magic of Stock Transaction Timing*.

HOW MOVING AVERAGES WORK

Many traders and investors have said that if they were forced to choose only one indicator, it would probably be moving averages. Even some investors who almost never look at indicators pay attention to moving averages. Why? Because this indicator is powerful yet easy to use and simple to understand on a chart.

Basically, moving averages show the value of a security's price over the duration of a period of time, such as the last 20, 50, 100, or 200 days. By overlaying the moving average on top of the stock or market, you get a good feel for the direction of the market. Traders who use trend-following strategies are drawn to moving averages. Also, when moving averages are displayed on a chart, it's much easier to see trend changes. For example, if the market falls below one of the moving averages, that could be a signal the current trend is ending.

Perhaps one of the best reasons to use moving averages is to help keep your emotions out of the trading process. For example, if you created a rule to buy when the market crossed above the 50-day moving average (and stayed there), and a rule to sell when the market crossed back below, you'd be surprised at what can be achieved. Sometimes it's hard to believe that a system so easy could be so profitable. Nevertheless, many traders tweak the defaults, using a variety of different time periods.

DECISIONS, DECISIONS

When you first select moving averages, you have a choice of seven types. Without going into all of the mathematical details, most people choose *simple* moving averages because it seems, well, simple.

For example, the 20-day simple moving average is calculated by taking an average of the last 20 days of the market's closing price and dividing by 20. So as the twenty-first day is added, the first day is dropped off. Put another way, old days are dropped as new days become available. It's constantly moving, which is why it's called a moving average. By repeating this procedure every day, a smooth line is created that can be displayed on a chart.

Another popular choice, the *exponential* moving average, is calculated in a similar way except that it gives a little more weight (18 percent, to be exact) to the last few days.

If given the choice between simple or exponential, you may want to choose exponential. Why? First, it's more accurate. And second, the simple moving average is a bit slower to respond than the exponential. (*Note:* If you're interested in learning more about exponential moving averages, go to Chapter 12 for a list of helpful resources.)

Another choice you have is deciding which moving average to display on the chart. If you're a short-term trader, you might use the 14-day or 20-day. For others, the 50-day, 100-day, and 200-day moving averages give a very good view of market direction.

Keep in mind that the shorter the time period, the more signals that are generated. You could think of the 20-day moving average as a quick and agile cheetah, while the 200-day moving average is as slow as a three-toed sloth.

THE ALMIGHTY 200-DAY MOVING AVERAGE

When the market crosses the 200-day moving average in either direction, this is considered a major signal. So many traders and investors follow the 200-day moving average that there is bound to be a reaction when a crossing occurs.

In addition, not just the 200-day moving average but other moving averages also act as *support* (which is like a floor) for the market on the way down. It's almost uncanny how the market or a stock can drop to certain support levels and remain there without falling farther. It takes a lot of selling pressure to move the market below the moving average.

And on the way up, other moving averages act as *resistance* (which is like a ceiling). In this case, it will take a lot of buying power to move the market above the moving average, especially the 200-day moving average.

NOBODY'S PERFECT

As powerful as moving averages are, they are not a silver bullet. Critics point out that moving averages are sometimes slow to react to market conditions. Remember that moving averages are called *lagging* indicators for a reason. Because they follow prices, they may give late signals.

For example, critics say, by the time the market has dropped below the 200-day moving average, you've already lost 20 percent. By that time, it's obvious to anyone the market is in a downtrend.

Proponents counter that moving averages weren't designed to catch the exact top or bottom but just to keep you on the right side of the market.

There is something else you should know about using moving averages: like any indicator, they don't work during all market environments. Moving averages give very valuable clues in a trending market. But in a trendless and occasionally choppy environment (also known as a *trading range*), moving averages aren't as effective. When the market is going nowhere, you might have to look for help with other market indicators.

STEP-BY-STEP: SELECTING THE 100-DAY EXPONENTIAL MOVING AVERAGE

Since we talked so much about exponential moving averages, in the short section below I'm going to show you how to change the default settings on a chart using StockCharts.com. (If you are an experienced user or if you are using your brokerage firm's software, you may skip this section.)

Specifically, we'll add a 100-day exponential moving average to the chart.

1. Open up www.stockcharts.com and type in **$SPX**.
2. Scroll below the chart to "Chart Attributes."

3. Note the default settings of "Daily (Periods)" and "Fill the Chart (Range)," and "Candlesticks (Type)," which you can change anytime.

4. In the "Overlays" section, click on the word "None."

5. A drop-down menu appears. Guess what? This is where other market indicators are hiding. (If you're not using StockCharts.com, the indicators are also hidden in a drop-down menu.)

6. Select the exponential moving average (EMA). The default parameter, 20-day moving average, appears. Click on the word "Update."

   Important: Whenever you make changes in StockCharts.com, you must click on "Update."

7. Scroll back to the middle of the chart. Notice that you have added a third line to the chart, a 20-day EMA. It's the green line.

8. Congratulations! Now that you know how to change the chart settings, you can change the defaults on any other chart.

For Short-Term Traders: The Moving Average Crossover Strategy

The straightforward but reliable *moving average crossover strategy* has been a favorite with traders for years. Although many short-term traders think they need complicated charts and lots of indicators, you can do very well if you follow this simple but elegant strategy.

The strategy is easy: You buy when the shorter 20-day moving average crosses *above* the longer 50-day moving average. You sell when the shorter 20-day moving average crosses *below* the longer 50-day moving average. Even if you're not a short-term trader, pay attention when moving average lines cross.

There is no rule, however, that says you have to use the 20-day and 50-day moving averages. Some traders use the 8-day and 13-day moving averages on a daily chart. Remember that the shorter the time period, the more signals you'll get, including more false signals.

Hint: Moving averages give other interesting clues. Watch the direction and slope of the moving average lines. Obviously, if the moving average lines are moving up, this is bullish. And if the moving average lines are moving down, this is bearish.

The death cross: When the 50-day moving average crosses under the 200-day moving average, it creates a cross that supposedly spells doom for the indexes. With such a mysterious name, *death cross*, how can the media ignore this signal? In fact, it can't. Whenever this signal appears, lots of articles appear warning investors to be careful. Author and hedge fund manager James Altucher ran a backtest going back to 1955 and found that if you follow this supposedly bearish signal, you will lose money 72 percent of the time. In fact, contrary to popular belief, Altucher says the death cross is actually a bullish signal. Nevertheless, if you encounter this scary-looking pattern on a chart, it could be a bad omen . . . or perhaps not.

WHAT'S NEXT?

Some of you may find moving averages so intriguing that you'll want to start using them immediately. There's nothing wrong with that; in fact, it's recommended you learn all the intimate details of each indicator you use.

Meanwhile, I'm going to introduce you to a very popular market indicator, MACD (Moving Average Convergence Divergence), which is based on moving averages. Even many investors who normally don't use technical indicators pay attention to MACD signals. In a few moments, you'll find out why.

MACD (MOVING AVERAGE CONVERGENCE DIVERGENCE)

Name: MACD (Moving Average Convergence Divergence)
Where to find: www.stockcharts.com or any chart program

Default settings: 12-day exponential moving average, 26-day exponential moving average, and a 9-day signal line (12,26,9)

Time period: Daily, weekly, or monthly

The Lighter Side: MACD, which I nicknamed "Uncle Mac," is like a reliable and trustworthy relative. If you follow its calm, long-term signals, especially at bottoms, it should lead you in the right direction.

WHAT MACD DOES

The MACD trend-following momentum indicator helps determine when a trend has ended or begun and may reverse direction.

STEP-BY-STEP: HOW TO READ MACD IN FIVE MINUTES

1. Type **www.stockcharts.com** in your Web address line (or open any chart program).
2. On the right side of the screen, type **$SPX**, which refers to the S&P 500 market index. Remember, you are also free to type **$INDU** (Dow Jones) or **$COMPQ** (Nasdaq Composite).
3. When the chart appears, look at the bottom of the screen. MACD automatically appears on the chart.
4. You will see two lines on the chart. The black line is referred to as the MACD line. The gray line (which often shows up as a red line on your computer screen) is referred to as the signal line. Simply put, there are two lines, an MACD line and a 9-day signal line. Keep your eye on the black MACD line! There is also a horizontal line that runs across the chart, which is referred to as the zero line (0 line).
5. It should look something like Figure 3.2.

WHAT SIGNALS TO LOOK FOR

1. **Buy:** When the MACD line (the black line) crosses above the zero line, that could be a signal to buy.

FIGURE 3.2

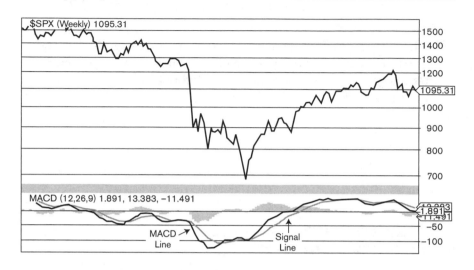

Source: StockCharts.com

2. **Sell:** When the MACD line crosses below the zero line, that could be a signal to sell.
3. **Buy:** When the MACD line crosses above the 9-day signal line (gray line on Figure 3.2), that could be a signal to buy.
4. **Sell:** When the MACD line crosses below the 9-day signal line, that could be a signal to sell.
5. **Note:** These are not actionable trades, but only guidelines. Always use other indicators to confirm before buying or selling.

THE BACK STORY

Gerald Appel created the widely followed MACD in 1976. At the time, before the personal computer, he programmed all of the algorithms into a calculator, attempting to produce a technical timing indicator based on moving averages that could signal traders when the current trend ended or began.

HOW MACD WORKS

MACD has a reliable history of giving few but well-timed long-term signals. Put another way, when many investors are hiding in cash and afraid to enter the market, the weekly or monthly MACD may suddenly perk up with a buy signal. The long-term buy signals don't appear often, but when they do, it's best to pay attention. It's your choice whether to set up MACD for a longer-term time frame (weekly or monthly) for fewer signals, or a shorter term (daily).

MACD BASICS

Because MACD can take a little time to understand, we'll go over the basics again. MACD usually consists of two lines: (1) a solid black line called the MACD line, and (2) a red line (sometimes dotted), called the 9-day signal line. The signal line is slower because technically it's a moving average of the MACD line. Yes, you heard that right: it's a moving average of a moving average.

The MACD line is the faster of the two lines. The reason you keep your eye on the faster MACD line is that it is the one that does the crossing. When the MACD line crosses above the 9-day signal line, this could be a buy signal. And if the MACD line crosses below the 9-day signal line, this could be a sell signal.

If you look at Figure 3.2, you'll also see a flat line called the zero line. When MACD crosses above or below the zero line, it generates a very reliable signal, according to many traders.

The way all of these lines crisscross, converge, and diverge with one another is what makes MACD so interesting—and so flexible—to traders.

CHANGING THE SETTINGS

Keep in mind that you have a lot of flexibility with time frames. If you only want to be notified of major signals, you can change the default time period from daily to weekly. And even more interesting, you can also change the default settings of (12,26,9) to match your trading strategies.

For example, scroll down below the chart to the MACD settings. Now change the settings to (19,39,9) and press "Update."

By making that little change, you have turned MACD from a short-term trading indicator to a longer-term trading indicator. By the way, Gerald Appel was the one who suggested you use these settings.

If you want to look at a much longer-term view of the market using MACD, you can double the settings from (12,26,9) to (24,52,18) on a weekly period. This was suggested by an acquaintance of mine who only wanted to be notified of major market signals. As you can guess, the (24,52,18) setting doesn't give many signals, but the crossover signal has been extremely reliable, especially at notifying traders when there is a market bottom. Obviously, the (19,39,9) setting for long-term signals is also reliable.

When you use market indicators, especially technical indicators such as MACD, you want to experiment with the settings. What you end up with depends on your goals and strategy.

NOBODY'S PERFECT

If only MACD were perfect! But it's not, unfortunately. Although the MACD crossover signal has had a good long-term history of picking bottoms, sometimes it gives confusing signals at market tops. Another criticism of MACD is that it can be somewhat slow at giving long-term signals. Even with these shortcomings, MACD keeps you on the right side of the trend more often than not.

STEP-BY-STEP: HOW TO CHANGE YOUR CHART SETTINGS

We talked a lot about changing the settings. If you're using a brokerage firm's chart program, call the Help Desk for directions on changing the default settings. If you are using StockCharts.com, here are the step-by-step instructions for changing the MACD chart settings:

1. A stock chart of $SPX or other index should be in front of you. You will see "MACD" displayed at the bottom of the chart.
2. Scroll lower until you see the MACD settings of (12,26,9) under "Indicators." (If you don't see "MACD," click on

one of the drop-down menus, select MACD, and press
the "Update" button.)

3. If you scroll back up a little, under "Range," click on the
drop-down menu. You can change the time period in the
range from 1 month to 3 years.

4. Click the "Update" button to save the changes.

5. **Advanced hint:** When you are ready, choose the MACD
Histogram indicator under the "Indicators" drop-down
menu. This gives you a visual representation of MACD
momentum. More information about the histogram follows.

For Short-Term Traders: Digging a Little Deeper

One of the reasons that MACD is so popular with traders is that it
combines the attributes of two indicators into one (trend-following
and momentum). Technically, the MACD line is actually the
difference between the closing prices of the first two exponential
moving averages, usually the 12- and 26-day (the 12-day less the
26-day exponential moving average is the MACD line). As
mentioned earlier, the 9-day signal line is a moving average of the
MACD line.

Short-term traders may want to change the default settings
to (6,19,9), as Appel suggested in his book *Power Tools for
Active Investors*.

In addition to buying or selling on crossovers, you may also
want to pay attention when MACD crosses above or below the
zero line. Appel says these signals tend to be very reliable when
buying or selling.

Another choice for traders is the MACD histogram (you can
find it on the drop-down menu on any chart program), developed
by Thomas Aspray. The histogram is similar to MACD but gives
you a visual representation of momentum in graphical form.
Histograms look like mountain ranges. As the "peaks and valleys"
get smaller, momentum is slowing down, which could signal a
change in direction. As the peaks and valleys get taller and
deeper, momentum may be increasing. It might also be signaling a
possible divergence.

Speaking of divergence, if the market moves down but the MACD line moves up, this could be a signal to buy. And if the market moves up but the MACD line moves down, this could be a signal to sell. Many traders believe that these kinds of divergences give reliable signals.

There are also some nuances about MACD that you should know: If you use the crossings of the zero line by MACD as your main signal, then MACD will work best in a trending market. However, if you use the crossings of the 9-period signal line as your main determinant, then MACD will probably do better in a neutral market that moves within large swings. MACD signal line crossings will not work well in a narrow, neutral market, but changes in the direction of the MACD line itself will. Although this can get a little confusing, keep in mind the indicator does have limitations.

Finally, some traders use MACD on multiple time frames and have three sets of charts: daily, weekly, and monthly. Use the longer-term time periods to study long-term trends, and the shorter time periods to look for buy and sell signals. (*Note:* A more detailed chart of MACD is in Chapter 12.)

If you're eager to learn more about MACD, then I'm pleased to introduce my next guest, Gerald Appel, psychoanalyst, trader, and the creator of MACD. He agreed to stop by and provide additional insights into how to best use his indicator and share some of the lessons he learned along the way.

GERALD APPEL: CREATOR, MOVING AVERAGE CONVERGENCE DIVERGENCE

WHY MACD IS SO POPULAR

In the mid-seventies, Gerald Appel was creating all kinds of timing indicators based on price momentum. Because the personal computer hadn't yet been invented, he'd program his calculations into a calculator. Finally, in 1976 he devised the Moving Average Convergence Divergence, or MACD.

"MACD didn't have that many calculations," Appel recalls. "I had friends coming in after school to help me enter the price into the spreadsheet and punch the machine." Back then, he says, it was quite an ordeal to make any progress. Fortunately, by 1980 he was able to automate the process by entering data into software.

Even now, MACD has remained one of the most popular market indicators for traders and investors. Perhaps the most surprised of all is Appel, who didn't expect the indicator to be so successful. Looking back, he thinks its popularity can be traced to how easy it is to maintain and how flexible it is: "It works because it's adaptable to any time frame. You can get a good reading of the major trend of the market by using MACD patterns that are based on monthly data. And you can also use it in a five-minute chart."

Appel says that if you look at MACD on a chart, it really stands out. "It's kind of intuitive," he says. "MACD is created by subtracting a shorter-term exponential moving average from a longer-term one. And then it takes an average of that. You can see when the trends are crossing their own moving average."

He says MACD gives the most precise signals at market bottoms. "It's more accurate at market low points than high points because of the way the market behaves," he says. "You can see it easily and readily. Market bottoms tend to be very sharp and pronounced, while tops can be a bit tricky. At bottoms, it makes very smooth lines, and you usually have climaxes and sharp reversals. It's a whole different feeling. A bear market can end on a dime, but a bull market doesn't. Market tops tend to be broad and slow. It's very possible for the market averages to keep drifting upward while more and more stocks are failing."

ALMOST PERFECT

Although MACD is as good as any indicator, especially when you backtest it, Appel warns it is not perfect: "No indicator is infallible. For instance, you might get a market rise and MACD turns down. Perhaps you think this is a sell signal. Well, it might not be a sell signal. A lot of times in a strong market MACD will keep hovering up in a high area, making little wiggles. It will flatten while the market is still going up." To avoid these kinds of false signals, Appel suggests not relying on any one indicator. "I would hate to put my life into any one single indicator, no matter what," he suggests.

To confirm an MACD bottom, Appel also looks at the New High–New Low indicator. "A diminution of new lows sometimes takes place even when the market averages are dropping down," he says. "You begin to see more and more stocks holding support. That's a pretty good indication that some significant reversal is going to take place in the stock market."

The opposite occurs at market tops, Appel says: "As long as the number of new issues making new highs keeps expanding, you're getting pretty good upside momentum. The number of new highs will decrease as the advance matures. The number of stocks participating and making new highs diminishes before the market averages turn down."

Appel says you want to use different parameters to help recognize a gradual shift in the market momentum: "If you are using MACD, I like to work with different time frames at the same time. Then all of the market events taking place begin to confirm together. But if you get a feeling the market is coming down and the short-term MACD begins to turn up, you want to see if it's a little blip or if you are getting changes in the intermediate MACD patterns. The more confluence you have, the better the chances you are going in the right direction."

And likewise, he says, as the market goes up and begins to turn, the shorter-term MACD begins to weaken first. Perhaps most important, don't make any sudden moves until you get confirmation from other indicators.

WHAT MACD DOES BEST

Although other people have made tremendous claims about MACD, Appel is humble about what it can do: "Basically, it gives you a picture of how market momentum is going," he says. "But there is a difference between price direction and momentum. In other words, if you're rising at a steep rate, you will see a lot of upside momentum. But suppose at some point, as it always does, the rise doesn't continue at that angle but continues at a slower angle. Perhaps MACD turns down, but stock prices aren't turning down. In that case, it becomes an early signal."

For long-term market trends, Appel says the monthly MACD patterns give good confirming signals about two or three months after a major bear market bottom is over. "As long as you try not to get in on the first day," he notes, "it could tell you it's time to get into the market."

Can MACD be used to forecast market direction? "I don't use it as a forecaster as much as a guide or compass," Appel says. "As long as MACD is falling, I stay away. I don't know how long it's going to fall. And if it's rising, and you see a bullish-looking pattern, I stay with it until it turns down. When the indicator changes, we change. We don't try to guess when the indicator is going to reverse."

HOW TO USE MACD

Appel suggests that people take the time to play with MACD to see how it works: "We recommend that you maintain two or three MACD patterns at one time. Since the market drops faster than it rises, we usually recommend a quicker-reacting MACD pattern for a buy signal. You could use a 10-day over a 20-day or 25-day pattern. At tops they seem to be more gradual, so you should slow them down a little bit, so we might use a 20-day over a 40-day. These are given in exponential numbers, so it would be 0.11 over 0.22 for buying, and 0.15 over 0.075 for selling."

He says that if you use a longer-term MACD, you can slow it down even more: "The question is whether you want to measure the intermediate or long term. If an intermediate term, you might use weekly patterns or just do it once a week. For short-term trading, you might want to use the daily MACD."

Usually, people at his firm use a top-down approach with MACD and other indicators to get a feel for the market. Then they will look at individual stocks they like that are trading well within that environment. In his office, they'll occasionally use the hourly MACD for very short-term trading.

USING MACD WITH MARKET CYCLES

Appel also likes to use MACD in conjunction with market cycles. He says that bear market bottoms tend to occur at four-year intervals. Tops have the same four-year interval. "A good timing frame is about six weeks apart in the stock market," Appel notes. "You have to have a feel for where in time you are. When the time and MACD pattern coincide, you have a signal you feel is reliable. If you find the four- to five-year cycle in the stock market, you can get a pretty good feel for when tops and bottoms will occur."

He adds that if you can put a calendar on MACD, you can see a somewhat regular pattern of low points that could give you an idea when the next one might occur. "It has clear patterns of when the market becomes oversold," he says, "when it's dropped as far as it can in terms of momentum, before recovering."

INDICATORS DON'T WORK FOREVER

At one time, Appel says, the fundamental indicator P/E (Price/ Earnings, the share price divided by earnings) was a pretty good indicator. "When the market was over 20 P/E, that was considered a sign stocks were too expensive and you had to be careful," he notes. "For decades people took this as the rule. But that went out the window in the 1990s. Stocks got up to 50 times earnings, and they stayed at higher levels."

He cautions that people are always looking for something to latch onto. "If something works in the stock market twice in a row, people get excited. They want to believe it's magic."

His suggestion: "The best advice I can give someone is to devise and follow a plan. Don't expect the plan to be perfect. There should be room for phasing in and out. But operate with a plan, because emotion will kill you. You want to try and make it as objective as possible. Never risk more than you can afford to lose, because that will create bad decisions. And diversify among a lot of different things."

In the end, he says that you have to admit you will be wrong, and not just a few times. "When you're wrong, take the loss. Don't let it build up, but try again the next time."

Gerald Appel, a trained psychoanalyst, who practiced for more than 35 years, became interested in technical analysis during the mid-1960s as he began to invest his own assets into the stock market. A self-taught technical analyst, he authored his first book, *Winning Market Systems*, in 1972, and he has since been writing books and articles, appearing on television, and creating the long-standing stock market newsletter "Systems and Forecasts," begun in 1973. The newsletter remains in publication, now edited by Marvin Appel, Gerald Appel's son. Gerald Appel is the founder and the president of Signalert Corp., an investment management company that employs many of the investment concepts that he has originated. Among Appel's more recent books are *Technical Analysis: Power Tools for Active Investors* and *Opportunity Investing*.

WHAT'S NEXT?

The next indicator you'll learn about, Bollinger Bands, is also very popular with traders, who have found creative ways to use it with the market as well as individual securities. This indicator is a little different from the others, one of the main reasons many traders keep it in their toolbox. They often use Bollinger Bands to confirm what they see with other indicators.

BOLLINGER BANDS

Name: Bollinger Bands

Where to find: www.stockcharts.com or almost any chart program

Default settings: 20-period moving average and two standard deviations (20,2)

Time period: Daily or weekly

The Lighter Side: Bollinger Bands, which I nicknamed "The Band," stretch and move as the stock price walks along an endlessly long and volatile road.

WHAT BOLLINGER BANDS DO

The Bollinger Bands indicator helps traders to identify overbought and oversold conditions.

STEP-BY-STEP: HOW TO READ
BOLLINGER BANDS IN FIVE MINUTES

1. Type **www.stockcharts.com** in your Web address line (or open any chart program).
2. On the right side of the screen, type **$SPX**, which is the symbol for the S&P 500.
3. When the chart is displayed, you should see a graph of $SPX for the last five months.
4. If you scroll a little lower, you'll notice the emboldened word, "Overlays." Click on the drop-down menu below "Overlays," and choose "Bollinger Bands."
5. **Hint:** Feel free to change the settings to make it easier to read. For example, remove "Moving Averages" and change the setting under "Type" to "Line."

The chart should look something like Figure 3.3. *Note:* This chart consists of four lines: price—the most volatile line—and the upper, middle, and lower Bollinger Bands. The middle Bollinger Band (the dotted line) is a simple moving average that is the base for the upper and lower bands and is used to describe the current trend.

Here are just a few of the signals you look for when looking at Bollinger Bands on a chart:

FIGURE 3.3

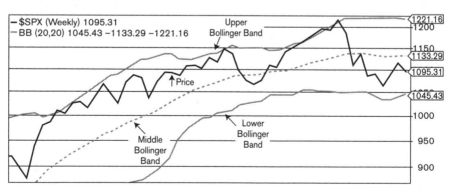

Source: StockCharts.com

1. **Overbought:** When the market (or stock) price pierces the upper band, that's an indication that the security is overbought.
2. **Oversold:** When the market (or stock) price pierces the lower band, that's an indication that the security is oversold.
3. **Note:** These are not actionable trades, but only guidelines. Always use other indicators to confirm before buying or selling.
4. **Advanced hint:** For a longer-term perspective, change the 20-day default setting to 20 weeks by changing the period on the chart from daily to weekly.

THE BACK STORY

Using a first-generation desktop computer in the 1980s, John Bollinger was an options trader who wanted to test the prevalent belief that volatility was a fixed number. Once he discovered that volatility was in actuality not fixed but dynamic and adaptable, he created Bollinger Bands.

HOW BOLLINGER BANDS WORK

Many traders like Bollinger Bands because they are flexible enough to be used on many types of securities, not just stocks. When you look at Bollinger Bands on a stock chart, you'll see an upper and lower band, most likely in blue or black.

There is also a dotted line in the middle between the bands. This is actually the default 20-day simple moving average. In addition, and this is important, you'll see the market price bouncing along between the upper and lower bands.

When the market price tags or pierces the upper band, it means that the market is overbought (i.e., there has been too much buying). What many people don't realize is that the market can remain overbought for some time before changing direction. Just because it touches the upper band doesn't mean it will suddenly reverse. Put another way, the market can remain overbought longer than you can remain solvent, to paraphrase economist John Maynard Keynes.

Conversely, if the market price tags or pierces the lower band, it means that the market is oversold (i.e., there has been too much selling). Once again, just because the price touches the lower band and remains there doesn't mean it will suddenly reverse. It can remain oversold for a long time.

If you observe Bollinger Bands long enough, you'll also notice that the market will linger along the upper or lower bands for a while. Many people get impatient when the market "walks the bands." Unfortunately, that is a misconception. The market could stay there indefinitely before turning around and heading toward the center.

That being said, often that's exactly what happens. The market will touch the upper or lower band and immediately reverse and head toward the center.

Some people might ask: Who cares if the market is over-bought or oversold?

I'm glad you asked! First of all, remember that in the default settings, Bollinger Bands are set for two standard deviations above the 20-day moving average. As you remember from a previous discussion, for the market to pierce the upper or lower bands, it must make a very strong move. After all, two standard deviations are well outside the norm. In other words, it is a warning sign. A market won't usually remain in that condition for too long before changing direction.

To answer the question above, although there are no guarantees, when you see that the market is overbought or oversold, it's time to pay attention. If other indicators corroborate what you see, then it could be time to take action.

IDENTIFYING MARKET VOLATILITY

Another signal that traders look for is the shape of the bands. For example, if the upper and lower bands suddenly contract (squeeze together), this is a clue that volatility is low. Don't be fooled by a quiet and low volatile market. When Bollinger Bands are very narrow, it is a signal the market could suddenly explode in the opposite direction. Put another way, periods of low volatility are often followed by periods of high volatility.

It works the other way too. If the bands are expanding, it means that the market is extremely volatile. There are no guarantees, but it's possible that the expanding Bollinger Bands is a signal that the market could reverse direction. The market doesn't usually remain in such a highly volatile period for long. Periods of high volatility are often followed by low volatility.

For Short-Term Traders

If you're a short-term trader, there are many other features that make Bollinger Bands so popular. Obviously, there isn't enough room to discuss them all, but I will leave you with this small nugget:

The upper and lower bands can also serve as support and resistance for individual stocks. If a stock breaks below support, it could mean the start of a downward trend. And if the stock breaks out above resistance, it could mean the start of an upward trend.

Advanced hint: John Bollinger has suggested that traders change the default settings. Instead of using the defaults of 20 and 2, you would use a 50-period moving average and 2.1 for the standard deviation. (*Note:* A chart of Bollinger Bands is located in Chapter 12.)

If you're thinking about the best way to use Bollinger Bands when trading stocks or indexes, then you'll be pleased to meet my next guest, trader and investor John Bollinger, who created Bollinger Bands. He stopped by to explain other creative ways to use his indicator.

JOHN BOLLINGER: CREATOR, BOLLINGER BANDS

UNDERSTANDING VOLATILITY

When John Bollinger started in the financial business in the early 1980s, percentage bands were wildly popular. "It was simply a moving average reflected above and below itself by some percentage," Bollinger recalls. "You might also have a line that was 7 percent above the average and another line that was 7 percent below the average. Those would be 7 percent percentage bands."

Although percentage bands are useful and many trading systems have been created using them, they have a number of problems. Bollinger explains: "By addressing those problems, I was led to create Bollinger Bands. The first problem was that you needed different width bands from stock to stock. Some stocks need bands that are 2 to 3 percent wide, and some stocks need bands that are 7 to 10 percent wide."

Because the bands varied, depending on the stock and time period, Bollinger said using them was very time consuming, primarily because you had to draw them by hand. Perhaps the worst problem with percentage bands, he says, was "they allowed your emotions to enter the trading process, which is a disaster, as we all know."

He says that percentage bands were designed based on data the trader wanted to include, a very subjective process. "I was looking for a system that could set the bands automatically," Bollinger says.

At the time, he was an options trader and was very concerned with how options were priced, which was based on calculating volatility: "In those days, we believed that volatility was a fixed number. We thought it was part of the property of a security."

In other words, once volatility was calculated for a security, it wouldn't be revised. "No one bothered to calculate it more than once a year, because it was believed that volatility didn't change," he says.

Fortunately, Bollinger had access to an early version of a spreadsheet called SuperCalc using the old CP/M [Control Program for Microcomputers] operating system. "One day I copied the volatility formula on the spreadsheet and saw for the first time that volatility was actually a dynamic number," he explains. "It was changing all the time. And I said, 'That's interesting!'"

That's when he realized he could use the volatility calculation to make the percentage bands more adaptive to real-life market conditions. "Over the course of a few months, with trial and error and different forms of volatility calculations, I came up with Bollinger Bands," notes Bollinger.

At the time, he knew he had a valuable tool, but he didn't think others would recognize it. "The way it was introduced to the public was through a television interview I did on the Financial News Network in the early 1980s," he says. "I showed a chart that had my indicator on it. I said we are projecting that the market will rally from the lower band to the upper band in a relatively short time. The interviewer asked me, 'What do you call those bands?' I actually didn't have a name for them, so I said, 'My trading bands.' Then I quickly blurted out, 'Bollinger Bands.' And that's how they got named."

CREATIVE USES OF BOLLINGER BANDS

It has amazed Bollinger the creative ways that people, including many option traders, have used his indicator. "People have reported using it in ways that I never imagined," he marvels. "I have received some tremendously good ideas from people who call in and say, 'Guess what I'm doing with the Bollinger Bands?' And I reply, 'Oh really? That's interesting, I hadn't thought of that one yet!'"

He admits his greatest joy in creating the indicators is the input he receives from other people who find original ways to use the bands. Perhaps the most surprising use of his indicator was from a man who approached him while at a conference in Japan.

Bollinger explains: "He showed me a graph in which he had plotted the Bollinger Bands on the equity line of a trading system. I told him, 'That's smart!' After that, I spent a lot of time using Bollinger Bands inside trading systems on the equity curves as an asset allocation mechanism."

One of the reasons that Bollinger Bands have remained popular is that they easily adapt to market conditions, he says. "The components of Bollinger Bands are trend and volatility. These are essential market forces. And they are depicted in a manner that is intuitively easy for people to grasp." He has seen all types of traders use his indicator, from people with no financial background to sophisticated mathematicians.

Other people have tried to create adaptive trading bands but none has worked as well, he notes. "You reach for the tool that works well. If you have a nail and a board, you reach for the hammer, even if there are other tools lying around."

THE PROPER USE OF BOLLINGER BANDS

Bollinger explains what his indicator actually does: "Bollinger Bands primarily tell you whether prices are high or low on a relative basis. Their best usage is to generate trading setups that can be used to calculate the probabilities that can then be acted upon. They create places where there is a high probability of success. When you find one of these places, you act at that time."

What they don't do, he cautions, is provide continuous advice: "Can you look at any given point in time at Bollinger Bands and know what to do? The answer, at least in my practice, is no."

He says that Bollinger Bands are not forecasting tools. They can't predict, for example, what the Dow will do on a certain date. Nevertheless, he acknowledges that within the Bollinger Band setups "there are obvious targets and obvious projections that can be made. It's especially useful to see whether a setup is working or not. But I wouldn't call that market forecasting."

One phenomenon that is unique to Bollinger Bands is that it tends to stay overbought or oversold for long time periods. "We call that a walk up the bands," he explains, "or a walk down the bands. It's perfectly normal. In fact, that is the sort of activity that is expected in a trending market. You may have to go for a long time, or a very short time, before you find a usable setup."

If someone gets impatient because there's no immediate buy or sell signal, he suggests it's a failure of the person, not the tool. He adds: "The biggest mistake that people make with my indicator is they assume that any tag of the upper band is an automatic sell, and that any tag of the lower band is an automatic buy. That's completely wrong."

Another problem is that people get fixated on certain signals even though the market is going against them. As a result, they go through a lot of pain. The key, Bollinger says, is to be flexible. Think of these trading bands as a component of a system analysis that also includes trend and sentiment information. "It's more useful to think of my trading bands as part of a whole trading system rather than try to be too simplistic."

EXPERIMENT OFTEN

In Bollinger's opinion, the best way to use his indicator is by experimenting with the defaults. "Fool around with the defaults as widely and creatively as possible," he suggests. "What could happen is you might stumble across something that works really well, a combination of rules or bands" that fits your trading style.

"Eventually you could find that sweet spot that works really well for you. One way to find it is by changing the moving averages from simple to exponential to weighted, or change the number of periods, or the number of bands. Then try it on 10-minute, daily, hourly, weekly, and monthly charts."

DEVIATION FROM THE EXPECTED

A concept that fascinates Bollinger is what he calls "the deviation from the expected." When you build a trading system, he says, you have an expectation that you will have at least 60 percent winners, for example. "And the winners will be about 1.5 times the size of the losers, and you'll rarely get a string of winners or losers greater than N or M." (N is the expectation of the average streak of winning trades, and M is the expectation of the length of the average losing streak.) He suggests that "you chart out each of these variables as your system goes along. And if any of them start to change, whether it's for better or for worse, you know that the character of the market is changing and that you may be in trouble."

The problem, Bollinger says, is that people ignore changes to their system if it's for the better. Why? "Because you're making money," he explains. "Let's say you steadily have 60 percent winners. Then suddenly over the next three months you have 65 or 70 percent winners. That's a deviation from the expected. That's telling you there's been a change, even though it's in your favor. It's as important as your going from 60 percent down to 50 percent."

But people ignore the change because it benefits them. "They only pay attention to the negative change, but each contains a warning that there has been a change in the underlying market."

AVOID A STALE TRADING SYSTEM

Although Bollinger did create a series of hard-and-fast rules for using his indicator, he discovered they didn't work out as well as he expected. "The markets morph and change over time. While one particular set of rules may work in one period, they fail to work or work in a contrary manner during another period," he says. "I found that the real value is to make my approach as adaptive as possible so the rules morph with the markets. This prevents you from getting caught with a stale trading system, one that is no longer viable for the market."

He explains that sometimes people create a trading system that tests well but fails when they try to use it in real time. "The proper use of out-of-sample testing in the development process can help avoid that," he suggests.

Although Bollinger says there is no way to avoid false signals, he closely monitors his indicators to make sure they don't get stale.

John Bollinger, CFA, CMT, is the president of Bollinger Capital Management, Inc. He is probably best known for his Bollinger Bands, which have been widely accepted and integrated into most of the analytical software currently in use. His book *Bollinger on Bollinger Bands* (McGraw-Hill, 2001) has been translated into seven languages. His newsletter *Capital Growth Letter* has been in publication since 1987. Bollinger is also the developer of several investor Web sites: www.bollingerbands.com, www.equitytrader.com, www.bollingeron bollingerbands.com, www.grouppower.com, www.bbforex.com, www .fundstrader.com, www.markettechnician.com, and www.pattern power.com. He is a speaker at financial conferences worldwide.

WHAT'S NEXT?

I hope you're still enjoying yourself because I'm now going to introduce you to a group of indicators called *oscillators*. The first one you'll learn about, Relative Strength Index, or RSI, is one of the most popular, primarily because it's easy to use and understand.

RSI, and its cousin, Stochastics, are referred to as oscillators because they oscillate, or move up and down between 0 and 100 on a chart. Although based on complex formulas, RSI and Stochastics are surprisingly easy to use. The difficulty, as always, is in correctly interpreting the signals. Generally, Stochastics and RSI are used to identify when an equity or index is overbought or oversold.

With these oscillators, when the signal line rises above a higher level, it is considered overbought. When it falls below a lower level, it is considered oversold. The theory: when a stock or index is overbought or oversold, it will eventually reverse direction. Many traders have profited from this deceivingly simple strategy.

Hold onto your seats, because oscillators have a reputation for being a little wild, but I'll do my best to give you a smooth ride.

RELATIVE STRENGTH INDEX

Name: Relative Strength Index (RSI)

Where to find: www.stockcharts.com or any chart program

Default settings: 14-day time period

Time period: Daily or weekly

Favorite market: Choppy

The Lighter Side: RSI, which I nicknamed "The Drama King," can be really unpredictable at times. If you follow this butterfly too closely, you can get whipsawed.

WHAT RSI DOES

The RSI indicator helps determine if the market or individual stocks have been overbought or oversold.

STEP-BY-STEP: HOW TO READ RSI IN FIVE MINUTES

1. Type **www.stockcharts.com** in your Web address line (or open any chart program).
2. On the right side of the screen, type **$SPX**, the S&P 500 index.
3. When the chart appears, "RSI" should appear in the indicator window at the top of the chart as a single line. (If it doesn't appear automatically, select "RSI" from the drop-down menu under the "Indicators" tab. Press the "Update" button.)
4. It should look something like Figure 3.4.

WHAT SIGNALS TO LOOK FOR

1. **Overbought:** If the RSI line rises above 70, that's an overbought signal.
2. **Oversold:** If the RSI line drops below 30, that's an oversold signal.

FIGURE   3.4

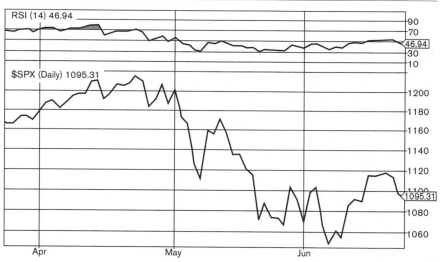

Source: StockCharts.com

3. **Note:** These are not actionable trades, but only guidelines. Always use other indicators to confirm before buying or selling.

4. **Hint:** For a longer-term perspective, change the period to "Weekly," and press "Update."

THE BACK STORY

J. Welles Wilder introduced the RSI in an article that appeared in *Commodities* magazine (now *Futures* magazine) in 1978. Wilder was an airplane mechanic and engineer who eventually became interested in using technical analysis to trade commodities. In addition to RSI, Wilder also created the Average True Range, Strength Index, and Directional Movement.

HOW RSI WORKS

RSI is a reliable indicator primarily used by short-term traders to try and catch the highs and lows of individual stocks. It seems to work best in a trading range, the kind of market that frustrates long-term investors. On the other hand, sharp traders can still find opportunities no matter what the environment.

Although preferred by short-term traders, RSI can also be used to monitor overbought or oversold market conditions, moving between 0 and 100. RSI is an oscillator, a special type of indicator that fluctuates above and below a centerline.

Beneath the surface, RSI is based on complicated formulas, but it appears easy to use, primarily because it has only one signal line. When RSI rises above 70, it's a signal the market or underlying stock is overbought. The tricky part, as you remember, is that the market can remain overbought for extended time periods. Some traders use an overbought reading as a potential danger signal. Conversely, when the RSI drops below 30, it's a signal the market or the underlying stock is oversold.

It takes some experience to use RSI because it tends to generate a lot of signals. If you want to master RSI (or its cousin, Stochastics), you'll need to do the following:

1. Experiment with the default settings.
2. Observe RSI in different market conditions.
3. Practice trading before committing real money based on its signals.

Once again, oscillators such as RSI tend to be used more with individual stocks for a short-term time frame, although it is adaptable to longer-term time periods. For some market watchers, the long-term RSI signals are perhaps the most valuable. Therefore, some traders change the default time period setting in RSI from daily to weekly to get a longer-term view of the market.

NOBODY'S PERFECT

Some traders think that as soon as RSI touches overbought or oversold territory, the stock or index might reverse. It's understandable why: After all, it takes strength for a security to become overbought and it takes weakness to become oversold. As mentioned previously, pay attention but don't expect an immediate reversal.

Also, depending on market conditions, don't get fixated on the 70 and 30 levels, as these may change depending on market conditions. Trader Alexander Elder explained it best; he wrote that *oversold* and *overbought* are like the hot and cold readings on a thermometer. The same temperature has different meanings in summer and winter. Therefore, during bull markets or bear markets, these levels might adjust upward or downward, respectively.

Another drawback: Depending on the settings you choose, RSI could go from generating multiple signals to moving between 30 and 70 without giving one significant signal. To solve this problem, start with the default 14-day RSI, but experiment with shorter (9-day) and longer (25-day) time frames to see how RSI reacts. Eventually you will find a setting that works for you.

For Short-Term Traders

One signal some traders look for is divergence. For example, if the market is making new highs but RSI is moving down, this is a significant bearish signal. Sometimes, the market may reverse, following RSI lower. Conversely, if the market is making new lows but RSI is moving up, it's possible the market will follow RSI higher. (*Caution:* Several traders claim that RSI divergences work less than 50 percent of the time, so tread carefully.)

Nevertheless, by looking for divergences on long-term charts, it's possible you'll identify major tops and bottoms. You should know that RSI, although a fairly good divergence indicator, is a bit slower to react than the next oscillator we'll discuss, Stochastics.

There are many other signals we didn't discuss here, such as failure swings and centerline crossovers. Learning how to properly interpret RSI signals takes a lot more study and experience than we have room for in this book.

Although RSI comes with a default of a 14-day period, many traders experiment with different settings. A 9-day period is popular with many short-term traders, and a 25-day period, recommended by Wilder, is favored by those who like to trade for the longer term. If you do use a shorter time period like the 9-day, or even shorter, it's possible you'll get a lot of false signals.

WHAT'S NEXT?

If you liked RSI, you'll love Stochastics, although it can be rowdy at times. Stochastics is a favorite with experienced traders, who like its precise signals. You should know that RSI and Stochastics can give almost identical signals, so you may not want to use both. Meanwhile, if RSI seemed too tame for you, then step right up: you're going on a Stochastics roller-coaster ride.

STOCHASTICS

Name: Stochastics

Where to find: www.stockcharts.com or any chart program

Default settings: 14 (%K), 3 (%D)

Time period: Daily or weekly

Favorite market: Choppy

The Lighter Side: Stochastics, originally nicknamed "The Drama Queen" by author and trader Toni Turner, is even more excitable than RSI. You'll need a firm and experienced hand to keep this duckling under control.

WHAT STOCHASTICS DOES

The Stochastics indicator, which moves between 0 to 100, helps determine if the market or individual stock is overbought or oversold, or if a trend is ending or beginning.

STEP-BY-STEP: HOW TO READ
STOCHASTICS IN FIVE MINUTES

1. Type **www.stockcharts.com** in your Web address line (or open any chart program).
2. On the right side of the screen, type **$SPX**, the S&P 500 index.
3. When the chart appears, click on one of the drop-down menus under "Indicators." Select "Slow Stochastics" from the list, and press the "Update" button. (*Hint:* If "RSI" is still listed under "Indicators," you can remove it by changing it to "None." It's not necessary to have both RSI and Stochastics on a chart).

FIGURE 3.5

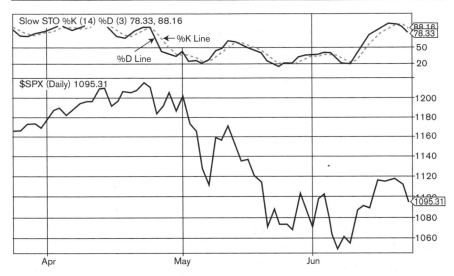

Source: StockCharts.com

4. Slow Stochastics will be located above or below the chart.
   It should look something like Figure 3.5.

WHAT SIGNALS TO LOOK FOR

1. **Overbought:** If the slower %D line (the solid black line)
   rises above 80, look for an opportunity to sell. *Note:* the
   dotted gray line (which might show up as red on the
   computer screen), is the faster %K line.
2. **Oversold:** If the slower %D line drops below 20, look for
   an opportunity to buy.
3. **Note:** These are not actionable trades, but only guidelines.
   Always use other indicators to confirm before buying or
   selling.
4. **Important hint:** *Overbought* and *oversold* are relative
   terms, depending on market conditions. The market can
   remain overbought or oversold for long time periods.
   Also, 80 and 20 are guidelines and may adjust upward or
   downward, depending on market conditions.

THE BACK STORY

Ralph Dystant, a Chicago dentist who also ran a technical analysis educators group, was reportedly the first to create Stochastics. After Dystant's untimely death, his teaching assistant, George Lane, continued to make improvements to the Stochastics formula, and he also wrote numerous articles on how to use it, thus making it even more popular. Tim Slater, who belonged to a group that helped develop numerous indicators in the 1970s, was the first to coin the name "Stochastics."

HOW STOCHASTICS WORKS

Stochastics is the favorite indicator of many short-term traders, but it's even more volatile than RSI. The reason? It's the formula: RSI uses only one line, while Stochastics uses two or three. Also, because RSI and Stochastics are so similar, many traders choose one of these oscillators but not both. One is not necessarily better than the other.

Many traders like Stochastics because it provides accurate and usually reliable overbought or oversold levels. It also helps traders identify when the current trend might end or begin. Keep in mind that Stochastics, although it can be used to generate market signals, is primarily used with individual stocks.

If this is your first experience with Stochastics, be ready, because this indicator generates a lot of signals. The following is a brief overview of some of the most important ones:

1. First, you'll notice that Stochastics is displayed as two lines, a %D (the slower line) and %K (the faster line). That's right, it comes in two speeds, slow and fast.

2. When you use Stochastics, keep your eye on the slower, black %D line. That is the line that will give you the most significant signals. And because it's slower, it will be less choppy and easier to use.

3. The most popular signal, as mentioned above, is when %D rises above 80 or drops below 20. This is significant, indicating that an index or individual stock is overbought or oversold.

As with other oscillators, Stochastics can remain overbought or oversold for long time periods. As mentioned with RSI, just because the market is in the "danger zone" doesn't mean it will reverse anytime soon. As one trader put it, some stocks or indexes can become "chronically" overbought or oversold. This may or may not be an actionable trade, but the security should be watched. Perhaps most important, be flexible with Stochastics and experiment with it before making a trade based on one of its signals.

When observing a stock or index price, if Stochastics closes near the highs (e.g., above 80), this could mean there is a short-term uptrend in the security. Conversely, if the stock or index price closes near the lows (e.g., below 25), it could signal a short-term downtrend.

In addition, many traders look to see if the two lines diverge. For example, if %D is moving down while the stock or market is moving up, it is possible that price might follow it downward. Conversely, if the stock or market price is moving down, but %D is moving up, that is a clue price might follow it upward. You will want to confirm the divergence by looking at other indicators. Unlike with RSI, divergent signals with Stochastics appear to be more reliable.

Hint: If you are a Stochastics novice, you might want to become experienced with the overbought and oversold signals first before you look for divergences. Then again, that's a decision only you can make.

NOBODY'S PERFECT

As with RSI, when Stochastics remains overbought or oversold for long time periods, it remains frustrating to many traders. In fact, then Stochastics could lose its edge, especially in trending markets. During a trending market environment, you'll want to confirm Stochastics with other indicators.

Stochastics signals have been misinterpreted in the past. For example, some authors incorrectly made hard-and-fast rules (an example of bad advice: sell when Stochastics goes above 80 or buy when it drops below 20), causing some readers to lose money. Just as with RSI, the Stochastics range shifts, depending on the type of market you're in.

The best advice this author can give is to use Stochastics with care. It's a superb tool that can be easily misused. To use this indicator properly, it's best to do your homework before investing real money into the market. If you'd like to learn more about Stochastics, go to Chapter 12 for additional resources.

Short-Term Signals

Stochastics comes in two speeds, fast and slow, with two (and sometimes three) signal lines, %D (the slower line) and %K (the faster line). Given the choice between Fast Stochastics or Slow Stochastics, you might want to start with Slow Stochastics. Why? It's easier, slower, and generates fewer signals. The downside is there is a slight signal lag when compared with Fast Stochastics. On the other hand, as a short-term trader, Fast Stochastics might be just what you're looking for.

Using Stochastics as a Trend Follower

Gregory Morris, author of *The Complete Guide to Market Breadth Indicators*, uses Stochastics in a different way than many traders. "Most people use Stochastics as a trading device," he says. "I use it as a trend measure. When the 14-day Stochastic is above 75, then you're in an uptrend. For a downtrend, it's below 25, a mirror image." He says that the uptrend remains in place until the Stochastic goes below 65 or 70.

"When Stochastics is above 75 and you're using a 14-day %D, you're in an uptrend," says Morris. "It's that simple. Remember that with every pullback, Stochastics will drop because it's measuring the last 14 days of the closing price."

Morris also smooths Stochastics with a moving average, which is similar to choosing Slow Stochastics. Smoothing simply means that you remove many of the jagged movements, which also generates fewer signals.

For Stochastic buy and sell signals, Morris looks for %D rising above 80, then dropping below 80. Likewise, when %D falls below 20 but then rises above 20, this could be a buy signal. Nevertheless, he cautions: "Don't ever forget that reading these indicators is an art form, not a science. If it were easy, then anyone could do it."

Another popular signal used by Morris and other traders is when Stochastic lines cross over the centerline, the so-called 50-yard line, as one trader referred to it.

Morris explains how to interpret the centerline. "When Stochastics is at 50 percent," he says, "it means that the closing price is halfway between the highest value and lowest value over the last 14 days. When it's at 80, it's 20 percent from the top and 80 percent from the bottom of that range. Although the Stochastics formula is scary, it's a very simple concept: You know that the price today is in the middle of the range of the last 14 days. The higher it goes, the more overbought it gets."

Using Stochastics as a Timing Tool

Alan Farley, author of *The Master Swing Trader*, uses Stochastics for 1- to 3-day swing trades, and uses RSI for a longer-term cycle. For Stochastics, his custom numbers are 5, 3, and 3. "It's very short term," Farley admits, "and is very noisy." One of the reasons he likes Stochastics more than RSI is it gives him the ability to smooth it out with moving averages.

"Stochastics is a very good derivative of price action," Farley says, "but I don't make buy or sell signals directly from Stochastics. I use it to pinpoint my timing. I am looking for a low-risk entry when the stock price is low. Then I put a stop right under the trading range."

As a swing trader, Farley is very focused on short-term 60-minute charts because it is about a day-and-a-half stochastic cycle. "When Stochastics turns higher for a day and a half, or lower for a day and a half, I want to line up on a long side trade. I'm trying to buy when Stochastics is near the oversold level and turning higher, or go short when it's near the overbought level and turning lower."

Farley also uses Stochastics as a way of keeping him out of trouble. For example, he won't buy a stock if %K and %D are separating, or diverging, from each other.

Although RSI and Stochastics are reliable indicators in nontrending markets, for most traders it's not necessary to use both. In fact, some traders overdo it. "Too many indicators are as bad as not having enough," Morris says. He suggests having a mixture of indicators such as price, breadth, and volume.

> When using indicators such as RSI and Stochastics, continue to practice and experiment until you find a combination of settings that not only makes sense to you but could also lead to actionable trades.
>
> Bestselling author and trader Toni Turner put it this way: "Indicators are like different instruments playing in a symphony orchestra. Although all of the instruments are different, when you listen to them, they all come out as a musical piece. But if even one of the instruments is playing out of tune, that is a signal you should pay attention to."

WHAT'S NEXT?

Before you leave this chapter, I'd like to introduce you to my next guest, Dr. Van Tharp, a trading coach and author who developed a number of indicators that help traders use psychology to understand the stock market. As you'll find out, he says your success as a trader depends on how well you know yourself.

DR. VAN THARP: CREATOR, ATR% AND SYSTEM QUALITY NUMBER

THE ATR% INDICATOR

Before Dr. Van Tharp's career as a psychologist, author, trading coach, and Market Wizard, he was a neurolinguistic programmer (NLP) modeler. For 25 years, he has been applying his research about NLP modeling to help traders think differently about the way they approach the market.

Each month, he monitors market volatility and direction. "I measure the volatility of the S&P 500 defined by a rolling 20-day average true range (ATR) as a percentage of the close, which I call ATR%," he says. "The mean of all of these 20-day windows over the last 60 years is about 1.31 percent, and the standard deviation is 0.72 percent."

When the ATR% is more than three standard deviations above the mean, he considers the market to be very volatile. "This extreme volatility only occurs in bear markets," he explains. "When the ATR% is between +0.5 and +3 standard deviations, the market is volatile. When the ATR% is between +0.5 and –0.5 standard deviations, the market has normal volatility. When the ATR% is less than –0.5 standard deviations, then the market is in quiet mode."

As a rule, he says, bull markets tend to range from quiet to volatile, and bear markets tend to be normal to very volatile.

THE SYSTEM QUALITY NUMBER INDICATOR

He also created an indicator that looks at the daily percent changes in the S&P 500 Index over the last 100 days using a proprietary technical indicator he calls the System Quality Number (SQN). (*Note:* A chart of SQN is located in Chapter 12.)

"I developed the SQN to measure how well trading systems perform, but I discovered I could also use it effectively to monitor what the market is doing," Tharp explains. For the last 60 years, he says, the market SQNs have ranged from +5, which is extremely bullish, to –2. "The negative numbers don't get as big because the SQN algorithm takes into account the variability of the market, which is always high in bear markets."

Although this might seem complicated to many people, he says that you can know the market type by just consulting a chart: "I use the market SQN as an indicator because I measure it every day, if I want to. The market SQN, however, is not meant to tell traders when to get in and out of the market. It's meant as a warning that you need different types of trading systems for different market conditions."

Tharp says that it's easy for anyone to develop a trading system for a single type of market. "Some buy-and-hold strategies worked well for growth stocks in the late 1990s' dot-com bull market," he says. "Unfortunately, when the bubble burst in 2000, people lost a lot of money holding onto stocks for the following few years. Buy and hold works great in certain market conditions, but it produces losses in other market conditions."

INDICATOR LIMITATIONS

Although Tharp creates and uses indicators, he understands their limitations. In fact, he says it's critical for traders to first identify and understand their beliefs about the indicators they use. "Let me state one of my primary beliefs about trading. You can only trade your beliefs about the market. The belief that I should enter or exit a trade based on some indicator is a very nebulous belief at best," he says.

Tharp illustrates how personal beliefs shape trading with an example of his own: "Because of my set of beliefs, I like to buy stocks that are going up without a lot of noise. I call these stocks 'efficient movers.' It stems from my belief that there is more profit potential in something that is going up and isn't too choppy than in something that is going up but is very choppy. As a result, I like to buy high in such trends and sell higher when the trend stops."

To find efficient stocks, Tharp has to look at price charts and see a steady trend. "I've never found an indicator that helps me find this kind of price pattern," he relates. "Indicators, in my opinion, tend to mask market action rather than clarify it."

For Tharp, looking at a stock chart is much more useful, as it helps him see the bigger picture.

SEEING THE BIGGER PICTURE

Tharp says that being able to see what the market is doing right now, and to feel the pulse of the market, will make you a better trader. To feel the pulse of the market, he relies on macroeconomic indicators such as Gross Domestic Product (GDP), job growth, and debt levels, besides just studying charts.

For the next several years, he foresees several deep economic crises, but it's still possible to find "plenty of ways to make money, although not with buy-and-hold strategies. It's important to observe what's going on at the time. It's important to have a good idea about the big picture so that you don't get confused when market conditions change suddenly. Prediction, however, has very little to do with making money."

THE SECRET TO SUCCESS

Tharp says, "There is only one secret to your success: You. You completely create your results, so if you don't master yourself, you'll never be a good trader—even if you have a great trading strategy."

He says that traders often make costly mistakes. "I define a trading mistake as not following your rules. And if you don't have any rules, then all of your trading might be a mistake."

He says that most traders make mistakes on three out of ten trades, which negates any profits they made on any good trading system. Why do traders make so many mistakes? Tharp feels that "most traders are unaware of how their psychology keeps them from making more money in the markets. Typically, you have to work at least six months to a year on psychological issues that cause you to make trading mistakes." Doing the psychological work up front, he says, helps minimize trading errors.

Tharp has seen high-performing trading systems that should have made it easy for traders to achieve money objectives. But, he observes, "Most people have personal issues that prevent them from developing these kinds of systems or trading them well."

It does help, he notes, if you have a certain personality type: "Those people who can readily perceive the big picture can more easily develop trading systems and seem to have a knack for trading. Those who get into lots of details and don't tend to see the big picture more often tend to be less successful traders."

He illustrates: "I could show you 50 examples of a stock going up after a green arrow appears on the screen. If you are a details person, and want lots of confirming data, you simply want to see lots of screens with green arrows. The big-picture person, on the other hand, will ask questions such as, 'How often will a trade fail when you get a green arrow?'"

It helps to understand your personality traits and trader type. The top personality for trading, according to Tharp, is a big-picture person who is organized and logical. Fun-loving personalities, however, would likely struggle with the tasks of trading: "The great thing about the fun-loving types is that trading probably doesn't appeal to them because it doesn't seem fun. We tell them they are better off having someone else manage their money." He even developed a test to help traders determine their trader type.

THE IMPORTANCE OF POSITION SIZING STRATEGIES

No matter what indicator or trading strategy you use, Tharp says it's essential you understand position sizing strategies to avoid unnecessary losses: "A simple and relatively safe position sizing method is to risk no more than 1 percent of your equity in each trade."

For example, with a $50,000 account, you'd risk no more than $500 in a trade. Continuing with this example: If you are willing to risk a price drop of $5 in one stock, you'd buy 100 shares. But to risk $10 on another stock, you'd only buy 50 shares. He explains: "In either case, the risk is $500, or 1 percent of equity."

At his workshops and in one of his books, Tharp has proven to participants using colored marbles that trading results have little to do with system performance; instead, they have everything to do with position sizing methods.

"Position sizing strategies are critically important for trading success," he says. "No one thinks about it this way, but an effective position sizing strategy is the single most important aspect of trading success behind personal psychology." In dollar terms, he claims that a trader's position sizing strategy accounts for 90 percent of trading success.

Dr. Van Tharp has been a trading coach for over 25 years. He is the author of *Super Trader, Trade Your Way to Financial Freedom, Safe Strategies for Financial Freedom, Financial Freedom through Electronic Day Trading*, and *The Definitive Guide to Position Sizing*. He publishes a free e-mail newsletter each week, including a monthly update on market conditions. That newsletter is available through his Web site, www.VanTharp.com. In addition, he gives numerous workshops and has an extensive Super Trader program for committed traders who want to take their trading to the next level.

WHAT'S NEXT?

If you are ready to go forward, you'll discover that the next chapter is a breeze. The indicators in Chapter 4 are just as popular as the ones you just read about, but they are quite different. I purposely decided to lighten things up a bit in Chapter 4, and for some of you, it may be the most entertaining part of the book.

CHAPTER 4

Outside the Box

Now that you've been introduced to traditional indicators, we'll discuss indicators that are outside the box but are still used by many traders to monitor the market. Some of these indicators may seem unusual, and a few are mysterious, but all give important clues to solving this puzzle we call the stock market.

CALENDAR-BASED INDICATORS

Calendar-based indicators and seasonal indicators are popular and easy to understand. For example, in the early 1980s, University of Chicago graduate student Donald Keim, now a professor of finance at the Wharton School of the University of Pennsylvania, first observed the phenomenon that small stocks outperform large stocks in January more than in other months. The pattern is hypothesized to be attributable to tax-related trading at the turn of the year. And for many years, this pattern persisted. Small stocks outperformed large stocks in January nearly every year from the late 1920s to the late 1980s.

Eventually, the idea turned into the so-called January Effect, coined by Keim. When January is weak, it's a bad omen. And if January is strong, it could be a good year for the stock market. The accuracy rate of the January Effect has generally been above average.

Over time, the January Effect lost some of its effectiveness as individuals and institutions stopped selling individual stocks at the end of the year and buying them back in January. Financial reporters continue to write about the January Effect, but as you'll read next, there are more reliable calendar-based indicators.

JANUARY: STILL THE MOST IMPORTANT MONTH OF THE YEAR

Of all the months, January is still the most significant. This is the month that sets the tone for the rest of the year, based on the results of several calendar-based trading systems. Also, according to a survey on market anomalies included in the *New Palgrave Dictionary of Economics*, Keim and others found that "50 percent of the annual size premium in the U.S. is concentrated in the month of January, particularly in the first week of the year."

Often confused with the January Effect is the powerful January Barometer. Unlike the January Effect, which refers to the difference in returns between small-cap and large-cap stocks, the January Barometer simply refers to the returns of the S&P 500 in January.

Devised by Yale Hirsch in 1972, the January Barometer has had a relatively good accuracy rate. The theory is that whatever happens to the S&P in January will set the mood for the rest of the year. "As the S&P goes in January, so goes the year," Hirsch wrote.

Here are the rules for using the January Barometer:

1. If the S&P is up in January, the market is likely to have an up year.
2. If the S&P is down in January, the market is likely to be flat or down for the year.

To learn more about forecasting market behavior based on calendar trends, the most popular annual resource is the *Stock Trader's Almanac* (Wiley), coauthored by Jeffrey Hirsch and Yale Hirsch.

The purpose of the book, according to Jeffrey Hirsch, is to help use calendar events and history for clues to the future. He explains: "The idea is to get people's minds around the market's calendar and the historical patterns it follows, from half-hourly trading patterns to four-year presidential stock market cycles." The book includes stock market facts, daily motivational quotes, and calendar-based rules such as the January Barometer.

"As a seasonal indicator, I think the January Barometer still shines brightly," Jeffrey Hirsch says. It's an indication of what the climate is for that year, he says, just one of many things you look at.

What if January is negative? "If you're a long-term investor," Hirsch says, "you'd want to be more cautious about making new purchases. Consider taking profits on rallies. If you're a short-term trader, you could implement hedge strategies or go short. You could also sell covered calls."

Jeffrey Hirsch admits that although the January Barometer is useful, sometimes it doesn't work. "There are times when the January Barometer has been less indicative, so you always have to consider other indicators before making a move into or out of the market."

A well-known calendar-based saying that has also been reliable is summarized by the old Wall Street adage, "Sell in May and go away." According to Hirsch, you should be invested in stocks between November 1 and April 30, and then switch to fixed income for the other six months. "This has produced reliable returns with reduced risk since 1950," Hirsch says.

He explains that "people's behavior and what they do with their money and time affects the economy and the stock market. This creates seasonal and other recurring patterns in the market."

But nothing works all the time, he cautions, "so you have to be attuned to current events and market conditions when using calendar indicators. Don't be the last bear or last bull standing. Let history guide you, be contrary to the crowd, and let the tape tell you when to act."

For example, for years you couldn't go wrong if you followed an obscure indicator called the "September Reverse Barometer." The theory: if the market was down in September, you'd invest after the September harvest when farmers invested their paychecks in the stock market. However, as people switched from working on farms to living in the city, the indicator permanently stopped working.

Therefore, if you do use calendar-based indicators, it's essential that you also consider technical and fundamental indicators before making big bets based on their results. In addition, pay close attention to how the market performs in January. Mark your calendar now.

MARKET CYCLES

After reading a number of interviews, you may have noticed that several traders mentioned they follow market cycles. The theory, which is well beyond the scope of this book, is that the stock market, just like the planet, goes through regular, predictable phases or cycles. (You'll sometimes hear traders refer to a *cyclical* bear market or *secular* bull market.)

By studying historical stock market patterns, traders who follow market cycles claim they can identify certain patterns that show up repeatedly on charts. This also includes recognized market stages such as *accumulation* (bottom), *mark up* (rise), *distribution* (top), and *markdown* (decline).

Although using market cycles is not a precise timing tool, it's also not a "mystical numerological scheme," as one trader put it. Those who follow market cycles say it's a phenomenon you should not ignore, especially if you want to avoid bear markets. The goal is to recognize which cycle the market is in so you can invest accordingly, but keep in mind that many of these cycles last dozens of years.

Although there appears to be some truth to the reliability of market cycles, it's recommended you conduct your own research. Unfortunately, you may discover that many of the market cycle newsletters that populate the Internet make outlandish predictions based on nothing more than astrological or numerical patterns— you could probably do better by visiting your local fortune-teller. *Suggestion:* Do your homework. If you are intrigued by market cycles, find out for yourself whether these concepts are valid.

You can also pick up a copy of the old classic *Extraordinary Popular Delusions and the Madness of Crowds* by Charles MacKay. After reading this book, you'll learn that human nature never seems to change. In fact, understanding how people react to booms and busts throughout history can give valuable insights into crowd psychology. Now this is a vicious cycle you can always rely on.

Another popular cycle is the investor sentiment cycle, which shows the various emotions that many investors experience as the market rises and falls. Author Justin Mamis was the first to come up with this idea back in the 1990s. I created my own version, which can be found in Figure 4.1. The idea is to use investor psychology and sentiment indicators (discussed in Chapter 7) to make predictions about what the market may do next.

FIGURE 4.1

Investor sentiment cycle

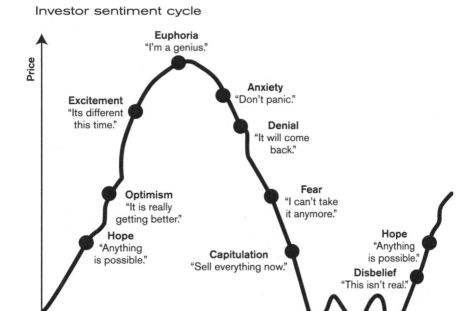

Source: www.michaelsincere.com

FIBONACCI

You're traveling to another dimension, a dimension not only of sight and sound, but of mind—a journey into a wondrous land whose boundaries are that of imagination. The signpost up ahead: Fibonacci.

All teasing aside, a number of extremely serious traders are devoted to the Fibonacci sequence, that mysterious indicator with a really cool name. Short-term traders primarily use it to identify key support and resistance areas. The support and resistance levels are based on the retracement of a previous move, either up or down.

You'll have to read a book or take classes to fully understand Fibonacci, but I'll do my best to summarize it. A brilliant thirteenth-century Italian mathematician, Leonardo Fibonacci, helped to promote a sequence of numbers that is the sum of the previous two numbers (starting with 0, the sequence is 0, 1, 1, 2, 3, 5, 8, 13, 21, 34, 55, until infinity). From this point, it gets even more complex, but Fibonacci sequences often appear in Renaissance architecture and art.

Traders who use Fibonacci are especially interested in 0.618, the "golden ratio," as well as 0.382 and 0.50. They will often set their stops right below or above these key levels. For example, stocks that are trending can suddenly fall back 38.2 percent, 50 percent, or 61.8 percent from their previous move before reversing. According to Fibonacci traders, if the *retracement* exceeds 61.8 percent, the current trend has ended.

Obviously, Fibonacci is not for everyone, especially since it can be so complex. If you are new to using market indicators, first learn the basics before you think about applying Fibonacci number sequences to a chart. Then again, telling people that you trade based on Fibonacci is so . . . mysterious.

ANECDOTAL INDICATORS

One of the most educational actions you can take as an investor is to observe other people. For example, in the middle of a previous housing bubble, people were day trading houses, college students were making $10,000 a month processing mortgages, and housing prices were doubling within a year. Few people seemed to realize the country was in the middle of a huge bubble.

The anecdotal evidence was everywhere, from a magazine cover of a guy hugging his house (the infamous *magazine cover indicator*) to lots of new real estate agents making fast deals over coffee at Starbucks. And yet, after the housing bubble popped, some of the smartest people in the country, including many government officials overseeing the economy, looked around and asked, "Who knew?"

You probably heard how Joseph Kennedy Sr. reportedly got out of the market because he received stock tips from the guy who shined his shoes. This anecdotal indicator suggests that when everyone is in the market and giving out tips, it's time to get out. Although anecdotal indicators are useful, it's often difficult to get the timing right. It could be years before a bubble or mania pops and everyone looks around and wonders what happened.

Another anecdotal signal you might think about is your dreams. Don't laugh, because listening to a dream saved me money: Several years ago, the stock market was moving higher and higher based on nothing more than greed and hope. As the market reached bubble proportions, few people thought it would ever go down. Like others, I had ridden the bull market to substantial profits and didn't consider selling, that is, until I had a vivid dream.

Briefly, I woke up in the middle of the night and thought I saw the New York Stock Exchange electronic ticker display board on my wall, red and green lights flashing. When I looked again, the ticker display board was covered in blood.

Instead of ignoring it, I reluctantly sold most of my stocks. A few months later, the stock market crashed. For the record, I've never had a dream like that again, but if I ever do, I'll pay attention.

And finally, as you probably know, every year somebody writes humorous stories about unusual anecdotal indicators such as the Hemline Index, the Boston Snow indicator, the Super Bowl indicator, the Sports Illustrated Swimsuit Edition indicator, the Presidential Winner indicator, and the Cardboard Box indicator (former Fed chairman Alan Greenspan was reportedly a fan of the last one).

Although a few of the anecdotal indicators mentioned above are logical, I personally don't think you should rely on any of them to make serious trading decisions—but you already knew that, right?

Way Outside the Box:
Check Hemlines or Count Boxes

Miami, Florida

I decided to find out for myself whether anecdotal indicators had any predictive power. For years, I had heard stories about Alan Greenspan's famous "Cardboard Box indicator." It was reported that he had made economic forecasts by tracking the demand for corrugated boxes. According to this theory, the higher the demand for the boxes, the more the economy will grow, and the better it will be for the stock market.

In addition to the Cardboard Box indicator, the financial media also drooled over the "Hemline Index," first observed by economist

George Taylor in 1926. It works like this: when women's hemlines (the line formed by the outside of a skirt) were shorter, it meant women were taking more risks, which encouraged spending, which is good for the economy and the stock market.

My deadline was approaching, and I had to find out if either of these indicators was valid. Obviously, I couldn't be in two places at the same time: I either had to attend a fashion show or count corrugated boxes.

At 9 p.m., I arrived at the Mercedes-Benz fashion show held at a luxury hotel in Miami. This was the real deal, a first-class event with a carpeted runway platform bolted on top of the main swimming pool. Photographers, a few movie stars, reporters, and models mingled with well-known designers. Someone cranked up the music as people found their seats.

I was on a very serious assignment to find out the truth about hemlines, which I explained to every model I met.

Just as I sat down near the front row, my assistant called me on my cell phone.

"I'm lost," she said.

"How hard is it to find a box factory?"

"Where are you?"

"I'm kind of busy," I replied. "I'll call you later."

The lights suddenly flickered; the first show was about to begin.

Men and women models walked along the brightly lit runway, heads held high, turning at just the precise moment as photographers snapped pictures. Although the models walked by rather quickly, I checked out the length of the women's hemlines. Conclusion: hemlines were very, very short. Forecast: next year is going to be great for the economy.

After 20 minutes, the show ended and most people went to the after party. My research had just begun.

My assistant called again. "I finally found the factory," she said.

"Good, how many boxes did you count?"

"Count? Are you kidding?"

Maybe I need a new assistant.

The after party was quite entertaining, especially the free food and drinks. I got a closer look at the models, most over six feet tall without high heels.

I gingerly approached one of the models. "Do you think your hemline can help me predict what the stock market will do?"

"Where are you from?" she asked without smiling.

"At the moment, from Mars."

"That's nice," she replied, looking away.

My assistant called again. "The factory manager said they had a really bad year."

If the Cardboard Box indicator was accurate, the economy was going down. I was confused. Which indicator was correct: hemlines or boxes?

"How many boxes did you count?"

"Two hundred so far," she replied.

"Two hundred? That's all?"

"You're mean," she said, and hung up.

To find out more about the Hemline Index, I spoke to Stephanie Solomon, a Bloomingdale's buyer and authority on women's fashion.

She told me some heartbreaking news. "The Hemline Index is a silly myth that has outlived its usefulness," she said.

"You mean the indicator is dead?" I asked.

"I hope so," Solomon quickly replied.

She explained that the length of a woman's hemline has little to do with the economy or the stock market. Back in the 1920s, hemline length was based on how much fabric was available, and not on the shopper's mood or desire to take risks.

I asked her if the bright and bold new designs at the fashion show meant that the economy was improving. Perhaps this was a leading indicator.

"Those are only trends," she explained, "just like high or low hemlines, and people will always purchase trends. It never falters. But there is no correlation between trends and what is going on in the economy."

"Is there anything in fashion that will help you make economic forecasts?" I asked.

"Absolutely," she said, "but you have to follow price. During a recession, if you don't have a lot of money, you'll buy the lowest price in the color of the moment. And when the economy is flush, you'll buy the same color but spend more money." She says that fashion insiders also know it's a recession because women stop buying designer clothes.

By the time I got home that night, I realized that financial reporters have to stop writing about the fun but insignificant Hemline Index, which has now become unfashionable.

Fortunately, I thought of a replacement, which I'm calling the "Fashion Indicator."

How does it work? Rather than study trends such as hemlines or color schemes, you watch shoppers, analyze clothes prices, and talk to designers for insights into how much money is being spent. It takes more investigative work but it's much more useful.

When designer labels become popular and people spend more money on clothes, it could be a very good year for the economy.

I can't wait to test out my new indicator at the next fashion show. Now that the Hemline Index is no longer valid, perhaps the Fashion Indicator can predict which way the economy is headed. I'll keep you updated on the results.

WHAT'S NEXT?

My next guest, prominent investor, *Forbes* columnist, and best-selling author Ken Fisher, stopped by to talk about what he learned from a lifetime of dueling with the stock market. He will also shed some light on an indicator he created, the Price/Sales Ratio, favored by many investors.

KEN FISHER:
CREATOR, PRICE/SALES RATIO

BEATING THE GREAT HUMILIATOR

One of the problems with indicators is that they don't always work in every market; even more frustrating, they sometimes stop working altogether. The lesson, says *Forbes* columnist and author Ken Fisher, is this: the market constantly changes, and so do indicators.

"The nature of capital markets is that things keep morphing," Fisher explains. "The market is analogous to a near-living spiritual entity that I refer to as the 'Great Humiliator,'" he quips. "It exists for one purpose and one purpose only: to humiliate as many people as possible for as many dollars as possible over the longest time period as possible."

Therefore, Fisher suggests, your goal is to try to minimize the degree to which you're humiliated: "And the only way to do that is to keep changing with the Great Humiliator." He says that many people have dug their feet in the sand and refuse to change their methods. "But my preference is to try and keep coming up with new things. Because in my industry if you're right 65 percent of the time, you become a legend—but it also means you could be wrong 35 percent of the time, which is a lot."

Fisher also says you have to be careful about making hard-and-fast rules. For example, he says you could make a rule to buy above a stock's 200-day moving average and sell when it's below its 200-day moving average. But it's not that simple. "The goal is to change with the world and come up with new ideas that other people haven't figured out yet," he says. "This also includes coming up with new market indicators.

"There are a thousand indicators," Fisher suggests. "All of these indicators have a time when they work and a time when they don't work. If you apply one set of indicators all of the time, you will by definition run hot and cold."

Fisher has tried out many technical indicators and found many inconsistencies: "Most technical indicators—not all, but most—tend to work sometimes and not work other times."

The key, he says, is to use them in conjunction with other methods: "You could look at MACD, which shows an oversold position. Then you could link that to a long-term fundamental indicator that makes you feel the economy is getting markedly stronger going forward. This gives you an approximate buy signal."

Fisher has other ways to try and beat the market. For instance, he attempts to figure out where the crowd sentiment is and matches that with economic reality: "If economic reality is different from sentiment, you try to arbitrage the spread between the two. The dilemma is that in the long run you have a laundry list of things to keep an eye out for, but as the world changes, you try and come up with new things that will work. I'm trying to get an edge by figuring out something other people haven't figured out yet."

Fisher is recognized for creating and popularizing the Price/Sales (P/S) Ratio, which has allowed investors to value a stock relative to its own past performance, other companies, or the market. Many have claimed the P/S Ratio has been even more useful than the P/E Ratio.

But things change, Fisher readily admits.

"I don't think the P/S Ratio has the power it used to have," he says. "When I was working on the P/S, there was no data written about it, so it was an exciting discovery. At the time, before the Internet, it was expensive to find the P/S of individual stocks."

Now, because you can get the P/S of almost any stock for free, and screen for it instantly, it's lost some of its luster. Fisher says it's the same with most indicators. They will work for a period of time and during certain markets. And then, just like that, they stop working, perhaps because more people find out about them.

LOOKING AT HISTORY FOR CLUES

According to Fisher, to be successful in the market, you should first learn how markets work. This means studying history but not totally relying on it. One idea is to study historical bull markets and bear markets for clues.

"In a bear market associated with a recession, consumer discretionary stocks usually get killed because of the fear of the consumer drying up," he says. "And when the bear market and recession are over, discretionary stocks bounce back very strong. That is pretty normal. In my many years in the industry, people forget that. When the economy is weaker than average, people always ask, 'Why would the consumer buy big-ticket items?'"

The answer, he says, is that people forget the market is a leading indicator: "Look at the classic consumer discretionary stocks—big-ticket items like luxury goods and cruise lines. It's hard for people to realize that when you're late in a bear market, once the bottom comes, consumer discretionary stocks do tremendous."

Although history gives insights into what could happen in the future, Fisher has some cautionary advice. "One part is to look at history, and the other part is not to rely on it," he quips. "History tells you what happened before, but as we move forward, history never does the exact same thing. The Great Humilator finds a way to twist it around."

Fisher is amused when people approach him with predictions of what's going to happen in the future. "I ask, 'Has this happened a lot in history? What do you base that on?' And if it never happened before in history, they are making a very strong statement."

Fisher says if that event happened a lot in the past, then maybe the statement is believable. "But if it has never happened before, you'd better have some powerful evidence to make me believe this event will happen. People tell me things all the time that are so improbable because they have happened so rarely in history. People who bet on the black swan will get their neck chipped."

BE CAUTIOUS OF COMPANY EARNINGS

Fisher wrote a book, *How to Smell a Rat*, about helping people to identify clues in advance when companies or financial advisors are unethical. Although he says that fraudulent companies such as WorldCom and Enron are relatively rare, there are some important lessons. "I don't believe you can have all that much faith in the earnings-per-share number that some company puts out," he notes. "I don't know if the accounting is that exact to begin with. Let me put it another way: The people who worked at Enron who had all of their life savings in Enron were unwise to take a double bet. I don't want to see my 401(k) invested in the company that I work for." To protect yourself, Fisher suggests that you diversify your investments.

He is aware that many people are looking for the ideal investment. "A journalist once called me up asking if I could recommend a security with an above-average return while maximizing capital preservation. I told her, 'There is no stock with above-average return while maximizing capital preservation.' It would be like having apple pie with none of the calories, a fat-free, calorie-free dessert. I'm not holding my breath."

Ken Fisher is best known for his writing the prestigious "Portfolio Strategy" column in *Forbes* magazine, where his 25+-year tenure of high-profile calls has made him the fourth longest-running columnist in *Forbes's* 90+-year history. Fisher is the founder, chairman, and CEO of Fisher Investments, an independent, global money management firm. He is on *Investment Advisor's* "30 for 30" list of the industry's 30 most influential people during the last 30 years; he is the award-winning author of numerous scholarly articles; and he has published six books, including *New York Times* and *Wall Street Journal* bestsellers *The Only Three Questions That Count*, *The Ten Roads to Riches*, and *How to Smell a Rat*. Fisher is number 289 on the 2009 *Forbes* 400 list of wealthiest Americans. He has been published, interviewed, and/or appeared in most major American, British, and German finance or business periodicals. He has a weekly column in *Focus Money*, Germany's leading finance magazine.

CONGRATULATIONS!

You have just finished Part One, which was sometimes challenging but was also the heart of the book. If you want, you can stop right now and experiment with the indicators you just learned about. Feel free to take a break, because you deserve it.

WHAT'S NEXT?

In the next section, Part Two, you'll learn how several trading pros use indicators to buy and sell stocks for a living. Perhaps now we'll find out whether it's really possible to use indicators to forecast the market.

PART TWO

How Traders Anticipate Market Direction

In this section, you'll be introduced to several traders who use a variety of indicators to enter or exit the market. All have a method that works for them, just as you'll eventually find a method that works for you.

It's one thing to read about market indicators in a book and another to use them in real life. In a traditional how-to book, everything works perfectly and everyone supposedly makes money. But in the real trading world, it can get messy. Sometimes indicators don't work as you thought, or the indicators work but you didn't make the trade. As most traders know, it's a lot harder when real money is at stake.

My next guest is Fred Hickey, who you briefly read about earlier on the first page of "The Opening." Hickey, a *Barron's* Roundtable participant and editor of a well-regarded newsletter, proudly trades the market from a contrarian viewpoint, which can be a bit lonely at times.

CHAPTER 5

Fred Hickey
The Contrarian

Hickey's Favorite Indicators

1. Investors Intelligence
2. CBOE Put/Call Ratio
3. Mutual Funds Cash Levels

DON'T FIGHT THE FED?

Fred Hickey put out a timely crash alert to his newsletter subscribers three months before the massive September 2008 crash, when the Dow ultimately fell below 6,500.

A few years earlier, he complained in his newsletter that the economy had begun to deteriorate. In 2007, however, it was impossible for Hickey to ignore what was happening. "The Bear Stearns collapse had occurred, housing inventories were up to an 18-year high, and prices were declining," Hickey says. "Mortgage brokers like Countrywide were laying off tens of thousands of people. The collapse was occurring in the economy, and no one was paying any attention to it."

In addition, the weapons of financial destruction, derivatives, had begun to detonate. "The credit markets had seized up," he says, ticking off a number of economic statistics that pointed to a possible crash.

What sidetracked many people, Hickey says, was the belief that the eight-member Federal Reserve (Fed) was omnipotent. "When the Fed cut rates, the market celebrated. People were euphoric, believing a rate cut would save them."

On TV, financial commentators were hooting and hollering, calling for another rate cut, Hickey remembers. "They thought the stock market would be immune. As long as the Fed was there, they believed the stock market would rally."

When the Fed surprised the market by cutting rates again, the same commentators called it a miracle, a gift from heaven, and the greatest central bank on earth. "One CNBC commentator was telling people to put their money into the Four Horsemen, including Google, at over $700 a share. When you write 'BUY GOOG' on your knuckles, that should give you some sense we're in trouble," he quips.

According to Hickey, many pros depend on the individual investors to fuel rallies. "Some of the antics you see are designed to lure greater fools with new money and short memories into the market."

Meanwhile, after the Fed cut rates, Google went even higher, even though it had missed its July numbers. "It missed its numbers because Internet traffic had started to slow," Hickey says. "And the biggest advertisers were from mortgage companies, who were going to get killed. And yet, they were on TV telling people to buy these high-priced tech stocks even after the fundamentals were rolling over."

Hickey is not a big fan of the Fed, which he believes has been irresponsible. "These are mostly Ivy League–educated economists, but they never get it right," he says. "Fed chairman Greenspan said it wasn't possible to identify bubbles, and yet there was this gigantic housing bubble that was obvious not just to me but to many people. Economists came out and said not to worry because the Fed had cut rates from 6 percent to 1 percent. But it didn't matter in the end."

He believes that the Fed members keep getting it wrong because they rely too heavily on their economic models, which never seem to come up with the right answer. "It's common sense versus economic modeling," Hickey says. "I was hitting my head against the wall. Why couldn't they see bubbles imploding all over the place?" Meanwhile, the Fed was supplying all this liquidity into the market by cutting rates lower and lower.

Hickey saw many similarities between 2007 and 2000. "According to market lore, you're not supposed to fight the Fed, but I knew it was time. History told me that. The Fed was not omnipotent in 1930, they weren't omnipotent in 2000, and they weren't omnipotent in 2007. I think it's very important to understand history. These patterns do reoccur, but not always in the same way. They are always a little different."

And just as in the past, people thought he was insane for fighting the Fed. "It wasn't just the crazies taunting me on the phone and singing songs," he says. "Legitimate people also called me and said, 'The Fed will never allow the stock market to fall because the consequences will be so awful. Stocks are destined to go higher. The Fed is too powerful. Resistance is futile.'"

BUBBLEMANIA

What was most amazing to Hickey, and also a clear sentiment indicator, was that people were willing to ignore facts such as earnings misses. "The evidence was right in their faces and people ignored it because other people were buying, and they expected other people to continue to buy. It was the Greater Fool theory."

As the stock market reached a new high of 14,000 in 2007, Hickey warned people that stocks were not immune if the housing market blew up. "And yet," he marvels, "the stock market continued to go higher." The volatility was extraordinary—another clue that the market was getting toppy.

Meanwhile, the economy continued to weaken. "There were all sorts of indicators that told me the economy was rolling over," he says. "FedEx, Lowe's, and Target saw declines in their shipments. I already knew the credit market was tightening, so money wasn't available for lending. This insane euphoria just couldn't last."

The pressure on Hickey to follow the herd was tremendous. When he told the *Barron's* Roundtable that he believed mortgage holders could be in trouble, one prominent member of the group snapped, "Poppycock!"

"It was a very difficult time," Hickey recalls. Only a couple of the Roundtable members agreed with his assessment of the economy.

Hickey also received calls from nervous fund managers who were under extreme pressure by clients to keep riding stocks higher. "I did a lot of hand-holding," he quips.

At the peak of the bull market, one fund manager moved his clients to a 35 percent cash position, an extreme defensive position by mutual fund standards. Because the general public doesn't usually like being in cash, this money manager was punished by numerous redemptions.

Not surprisingly, another indicator Hickey watches is mutual fund and hedge fund cash levels. "When fund cash levels go to low levels (less than 5 percent), it's time to be wary. And when they go to high levels, you have fuel for a rally."

To cope with the stress, Hickey turned off his computer, stopped watching financial programs, and focused on keeping sane. In his mind, the lunatics had taken over the asylum.

By the last quarter of 2007, Hickey was convinced people were making the same mistakes as before. "We were as blind drunk in 2007 as we were in 2001. I've lived through that already. There was no correlation between investors' perception of the market and reality."

And then, beginning in September 2008, the market crashed.

"It was a lucky call," Hickey claims. "You never know how high the market is going to go. No one does. But the market was too dangerous for me, and you can know when the market is dangerous, and it's time to get out. That I can do."

Looking back, Hickey wonders how this insanity could have occurred. "You couldn't make this stuff up," Hickey quips, also the title of one of his newsletters. People still believed that they couldn't lose money when the Fed was on their side.

Although Hickey timed the 2008 crash perfectly, in 1999 he got out of the tech bubble a bit early. "I will never regret that decision. There is nothing wrong in being too early. You just don't want to be too late. You also want to ride it until the train gets too crowded, and then you have to get off. If you're lucky, you'll get off at the right time, as was the case in 2008, but not in 2000."

THE CONTRARIAN VIEW

Hickey relishes the fact he observes market behavior in remote New Hampshire, many miles away from Wall Street. He believes that being away from the financial center allows him to see things more clearly. Nevertheless, he relies on a number of sentiment indicators, especially the Investors Intelligence numbers.

"The Investors Intelligence numbers always go to extreme euphoria," he says, before market tops or bottoms. "It will go 60 percent or higher on the bullish side when you're close to a top. On the flipside, if you get a huge number of bears, 50 to 60 percent, you might have a bottom." To avoid false signals, he suggests looking at the Investors Intelligence numbers over a long time period.

Hickey admits it's emotionally difficult going against the crowd. "I probably question myself 365 days a year. I always have doubts. It helps to have a support structure of people you have confidence in, who think like you do. It helps you through those tough times."

He also believes that individuals have a huge advantage over the pros. "It's far easier for individuals to take a contrarian stance than professional money managers. I don't think many people understand that."

GETTING THE RIGHT ADVICE

"Where do I learn from?" Hickey asks. "You don't usually learn from watching television. You learn from listening to people who have great track records. Read *Barron's* for people who have been right."

If you do get advice from a broker or money manager, he says you want an experienced mentor like Lou Mannheim, the stockbroker played by Hal Holbrook in the movie *Wall Street*. After Bud Fox, a young and overly ambitious stockbroker, made a killing in the market one day, Lou took Fox aside and said, "Kid, you're on a roll. Enjoy it while it lasts, 'cause it never does."

"People like Lou exist," Hickey says. "I know some of them. They're not the best performers because they're not selling you everything. They put their clients first, which means they earn less money than the others. These are the kind of people you want to find, but it's not easy."

On the other hand, Hickey says, some Wall Street folks are no better than used car salespeople: "They will sell you whatever is popular and whatever is hot, whatever will make them the most money. It's rare to find a salesperson who tells you to go into a money market account until the troubles pass. But these people are out there."

CLUES WE'RE AT THE BOTTOM

Although Hickey is known for spotting tops, he also looks for clues of a major bottom. "It's an educational process. I read everything that I can. A lot of it is experience. I am always learning." Connecting the dots, says Hickey, takes a lot of hard work. "I do this every day of the year."

To be successful, Hickey says, you have to be contrarian on either side of the market. After the market ultimately crashed in 2008, he sensed the doom and gloom on Wall Street and went long a number of tech stocks.

When the market has reached a bottom, he'll look for some of the following clues: "Sentiment indicators like Investors Intelligence will become extremely bearish, a signal to do the opposite. There will be a tremendous amount of put buying. Mutual fund cash levels will be extremely high, which will add fuel to the market. Historically, dividend yields are 6 percent, and the Price/Earnings (P/E) Ratio will be in the single digits."

In addition, he quips, "we've reached a bottom when there is no interest in the stock market whatsoever, and financial television programs become the senior golf channel."

Fred Hickey has been the editor and publisher of *The High-Tech Strategist*, which has offered an independent, and often contrarian, view of the stock market, economy, and technology stocks for the past 23 years. Fred has also been a member of the famed *Barron's* Roundtable since 2005. *Barron's* Alan Abelson has called Fred "the smartest guy on techs" and his newsletter "invaluable." After a brief stint as a sell-side analyst with a Boston-based technology boutique brokerage firm, Fred left to devote himself full time to his newsletter in 1992, which he publishes from Nashua, New Hampshire, and where he lives with his wife, Kathy, and his two children. Though he only occasionally grants requests for interviews, Fred is proud to note that he has turned down requests to appear on CNBC for 16 consecutive years, which he often refers to as "BubbleVision."

What Are Mutual Fund Cash Levels?

A number of traders mentioned they look at mutual fund cash levels to get a feel for how much cash the fund companies are holding. The contrarian viewpoint is this: If all of the fund companies combined are holding a lot of cash (e.g., higher than 10 percent), it could be a market bottom because they are investing so conservatively. Conversely, if all of the fund companies combined are holding little cash (e.g., less than 5 percent), that could be a top because they are investing so fearlessly. As with other contrarian sentiment indicators, the idea is that you do the opposite of the crowd, including mutual fund companies.

First, keep in mind the data is posted every month but with a one-month lag. Second, occasionally there are complex technical issues that can skew the results. Therefore, if you do look at this data, be sure to look for a trend and not an absolute number. Mutual fund cash levels should be viewed as one more piece of the puzzle.

Nevertheless, if you are interested in looking up how much cash mutual funds are holding, how much new money is coming in, and where that money is going each month, there is a company that keeps these statistics: Investment Company Institute.

The mutual fund cash levels are expressed as a percentage. Go to the Investment Company Institute Web site, www.ici.org, and click on "Research and Statistics" on the left side of the home page. Then click the "Statistics" tab in the middle of the page toward the right. Click on "Monthly Trends in Mutual Fund Investing." Toward the bottom, under the heading "Liquid Assets of Stock Mutual Funds," you will see the percentage.

As you have read, some traders think this information is very useful as a sentiment indicator. Although it's interesting, only you can determine if it's helpful.

WHAT'S NEXT?

My next guest is Linda Raschke, a professional trader and Market Wizard. As a Wall Street veteran, Raschke relies heavily on her experience, intuition, and charts, which she agreed to discuss in more detail.

CHAPTER 6

Linda Raschke
The Technician

Raschke's Favorite Indicators
1. Investors Intelligence
2. CBOE Put/Call Ratio

FORGET ABOUT FORECASTING

Although Market Wizard Linda Raschke uses a handful of indicators and has successfully timed the market to go long and short, she doesn't believe anyone can predict how far a market can really go. "Nobody knows how high or low something can go because markets tend to go farther than you think on the upside and farther than you think on the downside," she explains.

No one can predict the extent of a correction or a rally, she says. "At some point, the longer you go without a 10 percent correction, ultimately the more likely we'll have one, but you don't know if it's going to be 7 percent or 20 percent. It's a waste of time trying to guess how severe it will be."

Nevertheless, Rashke uses indicators to assess whether she should be long, short, or completely out of the market.

START WITH THE BASICS

Raschke stresses that before you begin to experiment with indicators, you should understand basic technical analysis, which means looking at and analyzing charts, support and resistance, price, and volume. She refers to the work of Richard Wyckoff, the legendary technician who studied charts and volume: "I think it's more important for people to understand the basic concepts of Wyckoff before buying a canned software program and having a zillion little squiggly lines. These are just tools, and tools can be misused."

She says that understanding the theories behind speculation, psychology, and price movement is much more important.

A good technician, she believes, needs a chart "so you can see where the highs and lows were made and how much the market rallied or pulled back. You're missing the point if you put too much emphasis on an oscillator without really understanding its limitations. Oscillators tend not to be as useful if you're in a really narrow trading range or a strong momentum environment. An oscillator can be overbought for an extended period of time—which can be a sign of strength."

She does consult indicators such as the RSI or a Moving Average Oscillator, but to her, they are all derived from price, which is the key to success in the market. "Pick any oscillator; they are all going to tell you the same thing," she says. "They are reflecting what's in the price. For example, if price sells off for five days, then the oscillators will be pulling down."

Properly using the basic tools, she insists, is essential. "The indicators are there to serve as confirmation. Your primary tool is to understand where you are in the market structure. This is far more important than only looking at oscillators like the RSI," she cautions.

Raschke adds: "Oscillators seem to get the newer traders into trouble more often than not, because the oscillator will be high and you might say, 'It should roll over and come back down.' It doesn't always work that way. An oscillator on a strong stock can get high and stay high for extended periods." The stock, she says, could be having a momentum move.

"You also need to assess trends," Raschke explains. "Is the market making higher highs and higher lows, or lower highs and lower lows? You also want to look at the volume that is accompanying those movements. You want to have a handle on what is the overall market structure."

Reading charts was one of the reasons Raschke accurately spotted the dangerous 2008 market. "The weekly and daily chart structure had been deteriorating and the market was making a series of lower highs and lower lows." She also began to see an increase of volume as the stock began to go lower. After analyzing all of the clues, she knew the market was in trouble.

"Everything works together," she says. "It's like the weather. You can't just look at the wind conditions coming from the east. You also need to know if you're in a high- or low-pressure zone. Just like in the market, you have to look at a combination of things."

And if a stock has been trading between 20 and 22 for the last two months, Raschke quips, "I don't need an indicator to tell me the stock has been trading at 20 to 22. And if it's starting to go to 23 and 24, making new highs, and breaking out from a two-month range, you can see it's breaking out from the chart formation."

SENTIMENT INDICATORS

In addition to reading charts, Raschke spends a lot of time studying sentiment indicators. "Aside from your technical toolbox, sentiment readings can be very useful in understanding if the market has upside or downside potential," she says.

"You can look at indicators like Investors Intelligence and the Put/Call Ratio," she continues. "In general, when everyone is bearish, the bearish sentiment has extreme readings, which is how a market bottom is created. When there are fairly high pessimistic sentiment readings, it means there is still a lot of cash that can be committed to the market."

Conversely, she says, the market will rally until there are overly bullish sentiments. "That usually means everybody has already bought." To get more clues, she suggests going on the Internet and looking at the historical sentiment readings for the last five or ten years to get an idea of how investors reacted in the past.

The idea is to understand crowd behavior. "We cannot predict the behavior of an individual," she says, "but we can predict the behavior of a crowd of people. It's a herd mentality. Crowds will tend to follow each other and want to do the same thing together."

Raschke notes there is a middle part where the crowds can be correct, but not for long. "You want to be careful when the crowd gets crowded," she says.

She explains this concept with the following example: "Let's say a stock has rallied up for two days. If you ask people about that stock, more than 50 percent will say it has an upside bias, that the stock is going higher the next day." There is a school of thought called *behavioral finance* that explains why people develop biases.

What is interesting, she says, is there is only a 50-50 chance the stock will be up the third day. "People have a built-in bias toward whatever the most recent movement was. These biases aren't necessarily grounded in logic or rational. In general, the decision making of most people tends to be flawed."

And it is this collective psychology, she notes, that repeatedly shows up as a pattern on a chart or in a sentiment reading. "When the sentiment readings begin hitting extremes in either direction, you want to be a contrarian," she recommends. "It doesn't mean you step in front of the train, but you look for other signs the market will go in the opposite direction."

Specifically, Raschke, as well as other traders, believes that the sentiment survey readings give important clues as to crowd psychology. It's also wise, she suggests, to listen to what the markets are telling you: "If all of a sudden you saw there was only a 20 percent bearish reading, that would be a warning sign everybody's already long. There's no new money coming into the market. You would assume the market was ripe for a correction."

Raschke says that obviously you wouldn't make trading decisions based solely on sentiment surveys, but you would want to consult the chart for other clues, such as support and resistance or a break in the trendline.

"Our job as traders is to analyze things and see if there are warning signs," Raschke says. "It's not a 100 percent science; there is definitely some art to it. But the art comes from experience. If a radiologist is reading an X ray, the more experience he has, the more confident he will feel in his diagnosis."

What you should be wary of, according to Raschke, is conducting your own informal interviews: "Just because the friends you hang out with lost their jobs and are gloomy doesn't mean that other people feel that way." And that's the whole point of studying the official sentiment polls and surveys, she says. They are more effective because they include a broad cross section of people, and not just your friends.

KEEPING AN OPEN MIND

Raschke has learned that to be successful in the market you need to keep an open mind. "I see people that get stuck on one side of the market or the other," she says. "There are people who are always bullish or always bearish. The biggest mistake people make is not being flexible and, perhaps more important, not admitting when they are wrong."

What amazes Raschke is that even after 30 years of professional trading, "every day I'm in the market I realize how much I don't know. I am learning something new every day." In the past, she never would have looked at global money flows, emerging markets, or the yield-curve relationship.

But she does now. "Things are always changing," she points out. Even if you're an investor, Raschke suggests, you should look at what the market is doing at least once a week. This means using indicators in conjunction with a bar chart. And finally, be aware of your own feelings, especially if you are feeling overly bearish or bullish. "Sometimes our feelings can be indicators as well," she adds.

Linda Raschke is president of LBRGroup, a registered commodity-trading advisor (CTA) and money management firm, and president of LBR Asset Management, a commodity pool operator. She began her professional trading career in 1981 as a market maker in equity options. Raschke was recognized in Jack Schwager's bestselling book *The New Market Wizards*, and she is also the author of the top-selling *Street Smarts: High Probability Short-Term Trading Strategies*. She has been featured in dozens of financial publications and on financial television and radio programs. Raschke was a past president of the American Association of Professional Technical Analysts and is currently on its board of directors.

Money Management 101

If there is anything that separates traders from their profits, it's money management. If you don't properly manage your money, the best indicators in the world won't help you.

The idea of money management is to minimize losses and increase gains. Obviously, this is easier said than done, but it can still be achieved. The following are a few techniques that traders use to contain potential losses.

1. **Be unemotional about money.** It's not easy to lose or make money without feeling something, but that's exactly what you may need to do. Although detaching yourself from money seems to go against your instincts, it's a helpful step. To reduce the emotional attachment to money, limit share size until you reach a comfortable level, use proper stops, and more than anything, learn to control your emotions when trading.

2. **Use proper stops.** Most traders have been grilled to use stop losses when trading, but if the stops are placed too tight, you could end up getting stopped out early and miss out on potential profits. Some pros recommend setting stops according to support and resistance levels, while others use arbitrary percentages. Try different methods until you find something that limits losses but doesn't stop out your winners too early.

3. **Ego is expensive.** It's fine to have a positive attitude, but if it turns into extreme overconfidence, it can be costly. You may have heard the saying that everyone thinks they're geniuses in a bull market. When entering the market, perhaps the only attitude you should have is neutral.

4. **Keep good records.** If you're trading, you'll need to keep good records, including a trading diary to keep track of mistakes. The biggest mistake of all is repeating previous mistakes. Avoid this by routinely reviewing good and bad trades, and finding ways to improve.

5. **Manage risk.** You may have heard this advice before, but it's worth repeating. Money management means managing risk.

This means starting small, calculating a stock's risk-reward before entering, and using less money to make more money.

6. **Determine your risk intolerance.** Before entering the market, you must be prepared to lose before you can win. Being a trader means subjecting yourself to emotional pain. Here's a quick risk tolerance test: What bothers you more, losing $1,000 or losing the opportunity to make $1,000? Your answer will help determine how much pain you can take when the markets unravel.

WHAT'S NEXT?

My next guest, Brett Steenbarger, a trading psychologist, author, and professor, agreed to share his creative insights and knowledge about using various market indicators with short-term trading strategies.

CHAPTER 7

Trading Psychologist Brett Steenbarger and Psychiatrist Alexander Elder, Creator of the Force Index

Steenbarger's Favorite Indicators
1. 20-day New High–New Low
2. 52-week New High–New Low
3. Advance-Decline Line
4. NYSE TICK
5. CBOE Put/Call Ratio

UNDERSTANDING WHAT INDICATORS CAN DO

As a trading psychologist, Brett Steenbarger relies on various indicators for long-term trading and short-term trading, and he even developed a few of his own. He also spends a lot of time educating people on how to use them properly. He says that although indicators give clues, contrary to what many people think, they are not a crystal ball.

"The goal of an indicator is to help people understand what is currently going on in the market," Steenbarger explains. "Indicators can tell you which way the wind is blowing. Although they provide useful information, in and of themselves they are not predictive. It's like the dashboard in your car, which is very helpful but won't necessarily predict the miles per hour your car might be a mile down the road."

What indicators can do, Steenbarger explains, is "to tell when a market is overbought and getting weak, and when a market is oversold and getting stronger. And that can lead to better decisions for traders to invest. If people really want to get started with indicators, they should observe them over time and see how they behave relative to the overall market and to individual stocks. As you follow these indicators you will recognize a recurring pattern, and this will be helpful in your decision making."

The goal, he says, is to take the time to learn everything about the indicator you choose, including learning all its nuances, both positive and negative.

THE 20-DAY NEW HIGH–NEW LOW

Steenbarger has personally found a number of indicators to be extremely helpful. "The first indicator I look at is the number of stocks making new highs versus the number of stocks making new lows," he says. "But unlike the standard New High–New Low indicator, which measures how many stocks have made 52-week lows, I want to see how many stocks have made 20-day new highs versus 20-day new lows."

He looks at both a short and intermediate time frame. "I want to see if a broad list of stocks is participating in a market move," Steenbarger explains. "If a lot of stocks are participating, then there could be some legs behind that move. If a smaller number of stocks are participating, then you'll see other stocks falling back and rolling over."

Steenbarger says that in a strong market that is going up, there will be a point when a maximum number of stocks have hit their 20-day highs, perhaps as many as 3,000 stocks. "Then the market will keep going up in price terms, but few stocks will participate. First you might see 2,500 stocks making 20-day highs, then maybe 1,600. So more stocks will drop off of the new high list even as the broad indexes such as the S&P 500 make new highs." For example, as the market topped out in 2007, fewer stocks were participating on the upside while others made new lows.

Because the S&P 500 is weighted more toward larger stocks, he says, the large-cap stocks could make new highs while the small-cap stocks drop off. "What this means is the underlying market is weakening even though the prices look firm. The 20-day New High–New Low indicator is a really nice alert for traders because it is more sensitive than the 52-week New High–New Low indicator." This is one reason why he tracks it in his own trading.

In addition, Steenbarger has found that the 20-day New High–New Low indicator can signal a possible collapse or even the beginning of a bull market. "This indicator shows when new stocks are participating or when fewer stocks are participating," he says. "This indicator is more sensitive so you can catch the little nuances of a strengthening or weakening market."

Steenbarger stresses that the 20-day indicator is best suited to shorter-term traders while the 52-week New High–New Low indicator makes more sense for longer-term investors.

SENTIMENT INDICATORS THAT WORK

Steenbarger relies heavily on sentiment indicators to assist with trading decisions. "A standard indicator I use is the Advance-Decline Line," Steenbarger says, "which is the number of stocks advancing versus the number of stocks declining. That is calculated on an intraday basis by many data feeds."

Steenbarger likes to use the Advance-Decline Line for particular indexes and sectors. "This gives you a sense of which sectors and indexes are relatively strong and weak," he says.

Looking back, the Advance-Decline Line emitted some clues prior to the crash of 2008 that something wasn't right. A large number of stocks were making new lows while the overall market was making new highs.

"Fewer and fewer stocks were participating on the upside as the market topped out in 2007," Steenbarger notes. "You don't make a forecast based on this one indicator, but in this case it tells you to be cautious. Then if you see a pattern played across a variety of indicators, it's a warning. That's when a lot of traders pull in their horns."

Conversely, when the stock market made fresh new lows in March 2009, fewer stocks made new lows, a sign of divergence. "Fewer stocks were participating to the downside while the market was making new lows," Steenbarger notes.

As it turned out, March 2009 was the low for the year. The S&P 500 subsequently zoomed up over 70 percent, leaving many frightened investors behind.

Another sentiment indicator that Steenbarger likes is the New York Stock Exchange (NYSE) TICK, a statistic put out by the NYSE. "It is simply the number of stocks that are trading on upticks minus the number of stocks that are trading on downticks," he says. "Obviously, if you have more stocks trading on upticks than downticks, it's showing you the buyers are being more aggressive." Conversely, if there is more trading on downticks than upticks, it's the sellers who are being more aggressive.

"This indicator is very useful for the short-term trader," Steenbarger says, but it can be combined from day to day to give you a longer time frame. "It tells the short-term trader which side of the market is more aggressive."

A third sentiment indicator Steenbarger likes is the CBOE Put/Call Ratio. This is the number of put options versus the number of call options. "A while back the Put/Call Ratio went as high as 0.80, which was an alert that the market was getting too bearish." And sure enough, the market proceeded to run up after hitting that peak. A few weeks later, the Put/Call Ratio fell to 0.43, which "indicated the market was getting a little bit toppy." It turned out to be a very good call.

STUDY THE BOND MARKET

In addition to the technical indicators that Steenbarger relies on, he pays attention to markets that are interconnected to the stock market, such as the fixed-income market. "You will see instances that high-yield bonds start to underperform high-quality bonds when the markets are getting a little frothy," he says. "And when markets are strengthening, you will see an appetite for risk. People will start buying the lower-quality bonds relative to the high-quality ones. That becomes a kind of sentiment gauge."

Steenbarger will also look at currency movements to determine the strength and weakness of various economies. "All of these intermarket relationships are quite important," he notes. "Are commodities strong or weak, or are we in an inflationary or deflationary environment? These are all very relevant."

DON'T FORGET ABOUT HISTORY

Another market gauge, if not an indicator, is historical patterns. "History gives you clues," Steenbarger says. "History doesn't repeat, but it rhymes. On a longer-term time frame, you can see these patterns. It helps to appreciate the bigger-picture moves that often occur throughout history."

An example was the crazy highs at the end of the 2000 bull market. "The tech stocks were flying off the pages, there was incredible optimism, and there was talk about it being a whole new economy," Steenbarger recalls. "That is the kind of ramped bullishness you get at a secular bull peak." It is similar to the phenomenal optimism in the mid to late 1960s. Just as in the 1960s, the decade after 2000 ended up with negative returns.

Traders like Steenbarger, who believe that history gives hints as to what might happen in the future, closely study market data and past market cycles going back to the late 1880s. "You try your best to be prepared for any possible scenario," Steenbarger says. "This goes beyond indicators, but once you have a framework of economic history, the indicators give you a sense of where we are in these cycles, and as the market gets stronger or weaker, you decide if you put chips on or off the table."

WHY GOOD TRADERS MAKE BAD MISTAKES

If your eyes gloss over because of all the indicators from which to choose, Steenbarger has some advice. "There is no reason to look at 100 indicators," Steenbarger quips. "If you have a watch, you always know the time of day. If you have two watches, you never know the time of day."

With too many indicators, he says you'll always find something that is contradictory. "Don't keep it simple, because there's a risk it will be simplistic, but keep it focused. Find the few indicators that speak to you, that make sense to you, and that you are willing to follow over time. Then you can internalize these indicators and get to know them intimately. I would rather follow 6 or 7 indicators and really learn their ins and outs rather than 30 in a casual fashion."

Some traders, especially beginners, don't always know what indicators are supposed to do. He gives this advice: "The indicator is like a reading a physician takes. A physician will read your blood pressure, take your temperature, and test your reflexes. But the physician has to interpret the data and put together a diagnosis. And that's what traders need to do: look at the indicators and other data, and put together a diagnosis of the market."

What novice traders often do instead, he cautions, is to "think that the indicator itself is the diagnosis and that it will make the decision for them. That just doesn't happen."

Because indicators are not as simplistic and mechanical as many people believe, Steenbarger thinks that some have gotten a bad name: "A physician wouldn't prescribe something by running only one test. So traders also shouldn't allocate their capital based on the results of one indicator."

THE WEIGHT OF THE EVIDENCE

To be an informed trader, you have to scratch beneath the surface and dig up information that is useful in that diagnostic process. "Just because an indicator is on a charting system or is mentioned doesn't mean it's an accurate decision guide," Steenbarger warns.

Obviously, there are no guarantees that any indicator is going to be foolproof. Steenbarger, like many traders, is looking for something more concrete. "I'm not looking for specific signals to make a decision," he says. "I'm looking for themes across indicators. You get so focused on what one indicator is saying and miss the broader themes. No indicator gives a precise prediction all the time, but I think if you look at the weight of the evidence, if you look across indicators, you can make some important decisions."

Brett Steenbarger, Ph.D., is clinical associate professor at SUNY Upstate Medical University and a coach of traders in proprietary firm, hedge fund, and bank settings. He has authored several books on trading psychology, including *The Daily Trading Coach: 101 Lessons for Becoming Your Own Trading Psychologist* (Wiley, 2009), as well as the TraderFeed blog (www.traderfeed.blogspot.com).

Masters of the Universe:
Long-Term Capital Management

If you've made a series of good trades and feel intoxicated with overconfidence, read this account of the rise and fall of Long-Term Capital Management (LTCM), the formerly profitable hedge fund managed by some of the smartest people in the country. Before it collapsed, it was considered the most impressive hedge fund in history.

Many of LTCM's managers had earned numerous degrees from some of the best schools in the country. At least two were Nobel Prize winners, and many were on the boards of the most prestigious brokerage firms. The people running LTCM were considered geniuses, and reading about their downfall teaches important lessons about trading stocks.

Let's start at the beginning.

At first, LTCM was incredibly successful, earning as much as 40 percent per year for its wealthy clients. At its height, it had over $100 billion in assets, much of it leveraged, including $6 billion in cash. As it made more money, its arrogance grew. People at LTCM were the masters of the universe, and in their minds, nothing could ever bring them down.

John Meriwether, their secretive but brilliant founder, handpicked a group of geeks who created complex mathematical computer models that traded bond derivatives. As their profits grew, they made bigger and bigger fixed-income bets using sophisticated trading strategies such as bond and merger arbitrage. Their complex models helped them to manage risk, or so they thought. Unfortunately, they failed to program one scenario: a once-in-a-million doomsday situation in which a huge country like Russia could default on its currency, the ruble. LTCM believed its computers would be able to forecast such a calamitous event.

Meanwhile, every year LTCM's partners wrote letters to their clients, which included how much they could theoretically lose; for example, 5 percent of their portfolio (the numerical odds, the partners wrote: no more than 12 times over the next 100 years, and only 1 year in 50 of losing 20 percent). Because LTCM was so confident of its positions, it was given obscene amounts of access to credit, which was used to leverage at a fantastic 100-to-1 ratio.

One of the flaws, which the partners didn't realize until it was too late, was there was no independent party to review or oversee LTCM's trading operations. Traders were given free rein to make any kind of trade they desired. And although the partners thought they had limited risk, they had unexpectedly created a scenario where risk was incalculable.

Although it was theoretically possible for their trades to "deviate from the norm," as the partners said, it was as likely as a "hundred-year storm." Perhaps their biggest mistake was not taking into account the twin emotions of fear and greed.

The end came rather quickly for LTCM. In August 1998, Russia's stock, bond, and currency markets went bust after Russia devalued the ruble, causing LTCM insurmountable losses. LTCM's computer models were not prepared to handle the level of fear and panic that spread across the world, as bond spreads widened to levels that no one at LTCM ever believed was possible. LTCM lost millions in equity as its cleverly designed trading schemes unraveled.

With the markets around the world in turmoil, LTCM made a desperate attempt to raise money, turning to billionaire investors like George Soros and Warren Buffett. Both men eventually declined to rescue the firm. The spreads continued to widen, and more millions were lost. In one month, LTCM had lost 44 percent of its capital, and 52 percent year-to-date, but that was just the beginning. The firm was hemorrhaging money as all of its investments went south; in addition option volatility skyrocketed, destroying its derivatives portfolio.

By the end of the year, on the verge of bankruptcy, the firm was taken over by a consortium of 14 banks. Several of the multimillionaire partners had already lost more than 90 percent of their wealth. "The Brightest and the Brokest," blared a headline from *Time* magazine. Other papers came up with clever headlines nearly celebrating the fact that a group of arrogant wizards could self-destruct so dramatically.

When the smoke cleared, LTCM had lost a staggering $5 billion in less than a year, leaving it with only $200 million to $300 million in equity, according to press reports. The professors, who ironically had designed their computer models to minimize risk, were probably shocked at how it all unraveled so quickly.

Although LTCM's meltdown occurred in 1998, what happened to it is a case study in risk mismanagement. In fact, a number of universities include LTCM as part of the curriculum. Business students study the hedge fund's collapse and identify the mistakes, as well as the lessons that can be learned.

One of the lessons: No matter how brilliant the system, there are unexpected events that can force the crowd to extremes and play havoc with your models. The professors learned the hard way that the stock market is not a mathematical experiment, or game, that performs as efficiently in real life as in the laboratory.

If you want to learn more details about the rise and fall of Long-Term Capital Management, read *When Genius Failed* by Roger Lowenstein.

WHAT'S NEXT?

My next guest is Dr. Alexander Elder, a seasoned trader, psychiatrist, and bestselling author, who was introduced earlier (Chapter 2). He'll discuss the indicator he created, the Force Index, in addition to sharing his ideas about the proper ways to use market indicators.

DR. ALEXANDER ELDER: CREATOR, FORCE INDEX

HOW THE FORCE INDEX WORKS

Dr. Alexander Elder believes in simplicity, which is why he limits himself to only a handful of indicators. "Most people's charts are very cluttered," Elder says. "I have a rule that I have only five bullets to a clip. A trader is allowed only five indicators. If you are really desperate, you can have six. But if you have seven, that is a problem."

The indicators Elder uses to monitor the overall market are MACD lines and histograms, moving averages, and envelopes. He also uses the Force Index, which he developed, to track individual stocks. "To me, the Force Index is the best indicator of volume. It brings volume to life. Looking at a bar chart of volume does not speak to me or to many other people. The Force Index turns those bars into a legible message." (*Note:* A chart of the Force Index is located in Chapter 12.)

"The Force Index works by combining three key factors," Elder says. "The direction of price change, the extent of the price change, and the amount of volume that it took to accomplish the price change."

The raw Force Index for any day equals price change times volume. "The greater the price change or the volume, the greater the Force Index. The Force Index can be positive or negative, depending on the direction of the market. Then we take this raw number and average it over a period of time." His favorite parameters are the 13-day moving average for long-term trends and the 2-day moving average for short-term timing.

HOW TO USE INDICATORS

Elder includes his main indicators on every chart combined with templates that cover the major time periods: weekly, daily, and intraday. For example, he likes to put *envelopes*, parallel lines above and below an exponential moving average, on his daily charts. "If the prices are hitting the upper envelope, I will not buy, no matter how attractive it appears. Occasionally, I will miss an up move because it will continue to have an upside breakout."

Since most breakouts are false, Elder says, he feels comfortable missing out on these setups. "You cannot win every time. When prices hit the upper envelope, they are overvalued. They can continue to go higher, but I'm not buying. I'm a value trader. I aim to buy below value and sell above value."

Each of his indicators serves a different purpose. "If you have a slow and steady uptrend, moving averages are perfect. But in a slow and steady trend, MACD stops working because it catches market swings. So I have learned over the years to recognize these factors. When a market is in a certain stage, certain indicators work better. They won't deliver magic, but they can tell you about probabilities."

It's essential you know the limits of your indicators. "Each indicator has its own set of rules," he explains. "It's like looking at a control panel in a car. The speedometer and the RPM meter give you different messages." The goal, he says, is to learn everything about the indicators you use.

BACKTESTING YOUR INDICATORS

Elder prefers to do manual backtesting. "I backtest by manually clicking on the indicator that I'm testing. At the same time, I have a spreadsheet open, so each time I have a signal I record it at that price level. This is the closest testing can come to actually trading."

Once he has tested a method manually, he will trade a small size using real money while recording everything in his trading diary. "In the nineties," he says, "I invented a strategy called the Impulse Trading System. The dream was to put my system on automatic and hire a kid to place orders and collect the checks. After manually testing the system for about 20 minutes, I realized I didn't account for slippage and commissions." Once he included these variables, the system was barely profitable.

"It took me a long time to figure out what was wrong with it," he laughs, "which I eventually did. I still use the system today."

Although not everyone has the time or patience to create his or her own indicators, Elder is adamant about this: "Most people don't create their own indicators, which is fine, but if you take someone else's indicator, you must personalize it for yourself."

By personalizing your indicators, you develop trading confidence, Elder says. "You don't have to invent indicators, but you definitely have to change parameters and fine-tune them for yourself. MACD is a wonderful indicator, but if you are using canned parameters, you've become a member of the market crowd."

Using the indicator defaults, Elder cautions, is ridiculous. "The basic premise is that the crowd will make money for a while but lose in the end. You have to do it differently. Crowds use the default values, so you should not use default values. Crowds fall in love with indicators but don't use stops. You shouldn't fall in love with indicators and you should use stops."

MONITORING HERD MENTALITY

Speaking of crowds, Elder always tries to figure out what the crowd is doing so he can go in the opposite direction at turning points. "There are many ways to track the crowd," he explains. "I read the New High–New Low Index every day. This is the single best leading indicator of the stock market. I'm looking to see if it's positive or negative, which tells me whether the bulls or bears are leading the market. I also look for divergences. If the market goes to new highs but the New High–New Low indicator traces a bearish divergence, that is a tremendously dangerous sign."

He manually updates the new high and new low numbers each day and plots them on a chart. "New highs and new lows are the leaders of the market, and I want to see what the leaders are doing," he adds.

He has other favorites. "I also look at the equity Put/Call Ratio. The Put/Call Ratio provides a very good view of what the gamblers are doing in the market." Dr. Elder copies the Put/Call data from the CBOE Web site and displays it on a chart. "I'm looking for the crowds to be extreme," he explains. "When the crowd becomes too bullish, you have to be careful about going long. And when the crowd is wildly fearful, that is usually a good time to be buying."

It's important to plot indicators such as the Put/Call Ratio on a chart so you "can see those long month-to-month waves," he says. He also puts *channels* (envelopes) on them: "Sometimes the indicators will go outside of the channels, which shows an extreme event is happening."

He cautions, however, that what might be an extreme event today might not be an extreme event in three months. That is another reason why he says that setting up strict parameters, or levels, doesn't make sense. "In bull and bear markets the numbers are quite different. They shift and change. That is why I compare them to their own history using channels."

Elder has other ways of monitoring the crowd, including checking what the public is writing on popular Web sites. Knowing what the crowd is feeling helps him with trading. "Crowds are correct in trends but they always miss reversals," Elder suggests. "Crowds don't believe when a bull market begins. Eventually they become believers and they make money on the upswing. When the bull market ends and the trend starts to go down, the crowd continues to buy. That's how they lose all of that money."

Another reason that people lose money when they trade is the lack of structure. "We are completely in control of our trades. This is a position that most people find stressful. There is no boss, no guidance, and no lines painted on the roadway. It is a completely unstructured environment."

People need indicators, Elder suggests, so they can have a sense of structure and discipline. "A disciplined trader is someone who paints his or her lines on the roadway. Using an indicator is like flying an airplane with instruments. If you are flying an airplane and you don't trust your instruments, you are going to get killed."

THE SECRET TO USING MARKET INDICATORS

"The secret to using market indicators is no different than in any profession," Elder explains. "The secret component is experience. As far as secret indicators, people don't have secret indicators as much as secret parameters. Most traders won't share their parameters. If you spend weeks playing with the length of a moving average and find something that really works, you won't broadcast that."

He says another secret to trading is mastering your emotions. "The intellectual demands of the financial markets are not that great," Elder explains, "but when it comes to the emotional aspects of trading, it's the hardest game in the world. People spend all of their time trying to figure out indicators, which shouldn't take very long. It's doing what your indicators tell you that people find extremely hard."

When your indicators throw you a curve ball, Elder says, you need good money management and risk control: "To me, every trade deserves three numbers: the price at which you enter, the price at which you take profits, and the price at which you get out. And if you don't have those three numbers, don't trade."

His final advice: "Trading is a wonderful journey but also one of the most challenging pursuits in the world. It's one of those things that people should get better at as they get older and gain experience."

Dr. Alexander Elder is a private trader and a teacher of traders based in New York City. He is the author of several international bestsellers: *Trading for a Living, Entries and Exits, Sell and Sell Short*, and *Come into My Trading Room*, named 2002 Book of the Year by *Barron's*. Elder was born in Leningrad and grew up in Estonia, where he entered medical school at the age of 16. At 23, while working as a ship's doctor, he jumped a Soviet ship in Africa and received political asylum in the United States. He worked as a psychiatrist in New York City and taught at Columbia University. His experience as a psychiatrist provided him with unique insight into the psychology of trading. Elder is the originator of the Spike group and of Traders' Camps—weeklong intensive courses for traders. He continues to trade, conducts Webinars for traders, and is a sought-after speaker at conferences in the United States and abroad.

WHAT'S NEXT?

Congratulations on finishing another section of the book. By now, you probably realize how important it is to manage your emotions when trading in the stock market. Even with the best indicator in the world, if you can't control your emotions, you could lose money.

In the next section, Part Three, you'll be introduced to various methods of looking at volume as well as a discussion on how high-frequency trading is changing all the rules.

PART THREE

Understanding Volume

OLD SCHOOL

Many traders say—as they do repeatedly throughout this book— that it's essential that you look at other indicators to confirm what the market is doing. One of these important indicators is volume. Because volume is the only indicator that isn't derived from price, it gives you a second opinion of the market.

Generally, you can look at volume by studying the volume bars found at the bottom of any chart. By combining volume with market indicators, you'll get a good feel for who is controlling the market. Perhaps price is the driver, but volume is the fuel that makes the market get from Point A to Point B.

Although there is a handful of volume indicators that appear on chart programs (On Balance Volume, or OBV, is used to monitor volume in individual stocks), many traders prefer to study volume directly. By studying volume, you can find important clues.

Nevertheless, you should also be aware that volume is going through tremendous changes. Because of the proliferation of high-frequency trading (HFT), some of the volume rules have to be modified. Later in this part, you'll read more about how these techniques are affecting the way traders view the market.

If you are not sure how to analyze volume, however, the sidebar below will give you a brief introduction.

For New Traders and Investors: Volume Basics

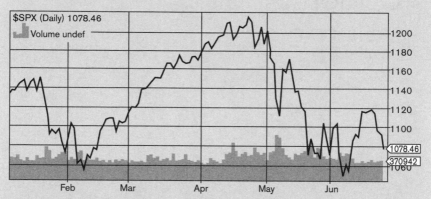

Source: StockCharts.com

Volume is simply the number of shares of stock traded over a given period. Sometimes you'll hear people talk about *liquidity*, which is how easy it is to get into and out of a stock.

Do you see the volume bars along the bottom of the chart? (Technically, it's a histogram.) For many traders and investors, those bars tell an incredible amount of information. There are several ways to look at volume. First, you can look up the daily volume of an individual stock or the entire market to see if it's higher or lower than previous days. Or, you can look at volume on a chart and follow the "bouncing bars."

Those bars are created by a computer, which collects all the *tick* (i.e., price movement) data, both upticks and downticks, and uses it to display a colorful volume bar. As volume goes higher and momentum increases, the volume bars rise. Conversely, as volume decreases and momentum decreases, the volume bars drop.

The general rule is that if the market rallies on higher volume, the move has broad-based support. Conversely, if the market sells off on higher volume, it could be a correction or *capitulation*. New buyers are afraid to step in.

Finally, although volume can be an important indicator, it's not perfect. For example, one problem is that you don't always know who is responsible for the increased volume: buyers or sellers. That's one reason why so many traders use volume in conjunction with other indicators.

One fact we know for sure: volume should not be ignored.

The Wyckoff Method

One of the first to recognize how critically important it is to study volume was Richard D. Wyckoff, a 1900s' trader and educator who worked with and analyzed the trades of the most successful investors and traders of his time, including Jesse Livermore, J. P. Morgan, and Andrew Carnegie. Eventually, Wyckoff's research of these successful traders and investors led him to create the Wyckoff Method.

Wyckoff's method involved studying bar charts, which can take a lot of time and practice to fully master. It's not just glancing at a bar chart and coming up with an instant analysis. Many of the concepts refer to his "Five-Step Method" and trading "laws."

For example, some of his guidelines include watching if the market is rising on high volume (bullish) or low volume (bearish). Conversely, you'd study if the market were falling on high volume (bearish) or low volume (bullish).

This includes looking for larger-than-normal volume to spot a trend change. Eventually, volume will increase so much that it creates what is called a "selling climax." At this point, when the unusual volume is so overwhelming, the current trend can end.

Wyckoff also stressed the importance of following the market trend, or individual stock. According to Wyckoff, prices follow the trend, what he calls the "line of least resistance": until something changes. Wyckoff then developed a number of sophisticated rules to define the trend.

Entire books and courses are taught studying Wyckoff's method, which can get very complex—even for experienced traders.

WHAT'S NEXT?

In the next chapter, *Investor's Business Daily*'s Kate Stalter will discuss how to determine stock direction based on tracking distribution days.

CHAPTER 8

Price and Volume

Based on the market research developed by founder William J. O'Neil, *Investor's Business Daily* (*IBD*) made a number of intriguing discoveries about price and volume. Perhaps most interesting, they confirmed that over three out of four stocks move in the direction of the overall market. Kate Stalter, market commentator at *IBD*, says, "Our research has found that the two key metrics you want to use are price and volume, especially institutional volume."

Stalter explains: "When you're looking at the major market indexes, and you see several days of heavy-volume selling within close proximity of each other, these big-volume down days are called 'distribution days.' When you see too many of those within a few weeks, you should take notice."

According to Stalter, stalling action, or heavy volume without further price progress up, is also counted as distribution. When the distribution day count grows to five or six over a five-week span, the general market almost always turns lower, she notes. (*Note:* A chart of distribution days is located in Chapter 12.)

"This is a proven historical signal going back to the 1880s," Stalter says, "that institutional investors are unloading their shares and the indexes are weakening. By the time you get to that fifth or sixth distribution day, it's a red flag. It doesn't mean you run out and sell everything, but it does mean you watch your portfolio like a hawk. The odds are no longer in your favor."

After that fifth or sixth distribution day, Stalter explains, *IBD*'s current outlook shifts to a market in correction. At that point, investors should avoid making new purchases. She says the best strategy is to continue tracking stocks outperforming the general market. "These stocks are often poised for strong uptrends when a new uptrend emerges again," she explains.

Speaking of uptrends, Stalter says *IBD* uses proven signals to change its outlook. "The research has proven time and time again you need several days of heavy-volume buying to confirm a new uptrend," Stalter explains.

Stalter says that *IBD* tracks market action that anybody can spot on a chart. "After one of the major indexes falls to a bottom," she notes, "watch for the first day for that index to close higher. That's day one of a new rally attempt."

Next, investors should look for confirmation of that rally. "That confirmation occurs on a follow-through day," she continues. "That typically happens on day four or later after a rally attempt begins, and it occurs as at least one of the indexes makes a significant price move in heavier volume than the previous session."

Nevertheless, Stalter says that investors have to use caution in the early days of a fledgling uptrend. "Although 70 percent of follow-through days work, it's perfectly normal historically for about 30 percent of new uptrends to fail," she cautions. "You just have to be prepared to sell any new buys quickly. If a follow-through day fizzles, it will usually happen quickly, within the first few days."

CHOOSING INDIVIDUAL STOCKS

As an investor or trader, the idea is to look at the overall market trend and use this information to buy individual stocks. "You want to know what the market outlook is," Stalter says. "Bucking the trend is difficult. You just create needless hassles if you do that. The best course of action whether the market is going higher or in a downtrend is to look at a stock chart. Once you know the market's direction, the key is to look at stocks that are actually showing leadership in that market."

IBD has other ways to compare individual stocks, including using an A-through-E rating system. "You definitely want to focus your research on stocks with the best ratings," she says. "Our researchers have found that stocks that outperform during a poor market are frequently the ones that make big price gains when the market's rally resumes."

In a downturn, Stalter suggests creating a watch list of fundamentally and technically strong stocks that could outperform when the market turns around. "When the market does turn around, be very choosy about which stocks to buy, and be ready to cut them quickly if market action is sputtering," she cautions.

Once again, Stalter says, the keys to determining if you're in an uptrend or downtrend are price and volume. "Professional investors account for the bulk of market action," she points out. "Institutions drive market direction."

Stalter has some final advice: "It takes a bit of time to master those rules, but it's worth it. And it pays to control emotions like fear and greed, so that's where having a set of buy and sell rules helps. That way, you can operate with a logical plan you adhere to in every market scenario. It's a whole lot better than relying on your own emotions, or even worse, listening to tips and opinions that you hear on TV."

Kate Stalter is a markets writer for *Investor's Business Daily* and host of the "Market Wrap" video at Investors.com. Since 2001, she has edited and written for *IBD* columns "The Real Most Active," "Stocks in the News," and "Investor's Corner." Stalter has cohosted Webcasts with TDAmeritrade and regularly presents at *IBD* investing seminars nationwide. She is an in-demand commentator on national radio programs. She received her MBA from the Kellogg School of Management at Northwestern University.

The Flash Crash

During the Flash Crash on May 6, 2010, the Dow Jones Industrial Average, already down by 161 points, plunged an additional 573 points within minutes. At another point during the day, it was down by 998 points. Just as quickly, it suddenly reversed and recovered 543 of the lost points. By the end of the day, the DJIA had only lost 347 points, or 3.20 percent from the prior day's close. Some individual stocks and exchange-traded funds (ETFs) experienced much wilder swings. For example, a few stocks went from $40 to a penny within minutes.

Flash traders, the likely culprits of the mysterious "Flash Crash," use high-speed electronic computers and questionable strategies to peek at other people's orders microseconds ahead of everyone else. Even though profits are usually a few pennies per share, all of these shares add up to billions of dollars per year.

After the minicrash, the NYSE and Nasdaq canceled approximately 19,000 trades made between 2:40 p.m. and 3:00 p.m. on that day. But many other trades were left as is, leaving thousands of unlucky investors holding dramatically lower-priced securities. According to reports, approximately 68 percent of the canceled trades included ETFs.

Buyers were nowhere to be found as other electronic traders simultaneously rushed toward the exits. Unlike market makers and specialists, electronic traders are not obligated to provide a fair and orderly market. In fact, it was also reported that many high-frequency traders turned off their computers, letting prices crash. Other professional "liquidity providers" also did not participate on the buy side, intensifying the price declines.

To critics, flash trading sounds suspiciously like front running. Many say that flash trading gives the owners an unfair edge over other market participants. It allows an elite group special access to quotes and the ability to determine supply and demand.

Proponents, on the other hand, claim that flash trading adds liquidity to the market.

There is little doubt that flash trading gives an informational edge, generating billions of dollars in profits each year, but is it fair?

Although high-frequency trading using high-speed computers is probably here to stay, the controversial strategy of using flash orders may be banned or regulated in the future. Until then, individual traders and investors may want to think twice before using market stop orders. If you had used a market order on the day of the Flash Crash, instead of getting stopped out at $50, for example, your stop order might have been executed at $20 or lower.

Meanwhile, as a result of this minicrash, new rules were proposed to "level the playing field." For many Wall Street old-timers, it probably feels like déjà vu. Although a flash crash is a relatively rare event, the promised reforms never seem to get past the various financial committees. In 2010, however, the SEC and CFTC (Commodity Futures Trading Commission) issued a joint report blaming the Flash Crash on a computerized trading program that automatically sold 35,000 e-mini S&P 500 futures contracts.

Eventually, new regulations will most likely be enacted, probably after the next crash. Ironically, it makes many yearn for the days when market makers and specialists controlled order flow, and the bid-ask spread was in fractions, not decimals.

In the opinion of this author, the last thing the market needs is the perception that a *Wizard of Oz* character is manipulating the markets behind the scenes. The sooner regulations are passed to make the markets fair for retail investors, the better.

WHAT'S NEXT?

My next guest, William J. O'Neil, bestselling author and founder of *Investor's Business Daily*, stopped by to share some of the lessons he has learned about being a successful trader and investor.

WILLIAM J. O'NEIL: LOOKING AT THE BIG PICTURE

William J. O'Neil, chairman and founder of *Investor's Business Daily* and Investors.com, has made a career of correctly anticipating stock market direction. When he first became interested in the stock market in the 1960s, he spent two years studying and researching how to be a successful trader. Because he had done his homework, he identified signals that a powerful bull market was about to begin. As a result, O'Neil turned $5,000 into $250,000 with a trio of exceptional trades. He continued studying the market, eventually using what he learned about indicators to launch *Investor's Business Daily*.

"The first book I read that helped me was *The Battle for Investment Survival* by Gerald Loeb," O'Neil recalls. "Loeb was a tape reader. He made $2 million pyramiding in Montgomery Ward while he was a young broker at E.F. Hutton. I also met with him several times."

O'Neil was also influenced by the market experiences of legendary trader Jesse Livermore as well as fund manager Jack Dreyfus. "Jack was a chartist," O'Neil recalls. "While he was active with his mutual fund, he did not use analysts but instead posted large oversized daily charts and had ticker tapes in every room of his office. He was always on top of the market action no matter where he was."

A MARKET INDICATOR THAT WORKS

O'Neil has advice for investors who are using market indicators: "Most investors like to follow different indicators, when in reality there is only one general market indicator we have found, cycle after cycle, to be dependable. In the stock market, three out of four stocks will decline when the major market indicators correct. These are the indicators we use to tell us when the general market is about to go south. They measure the general market more precisely."

Before he discovered the one market indicator that he believed was the most reliable, he analyzed all the different indicators known at that time. O'Neil notes that they created the method "many years ago after testing and throwing out virtually all other technical market indicators, which can work from time to time, but not on a consistent basis."

What he learned works best is following a daily chart that shows price and volume, day by day, of the major market indexes. "A market top starts when one index runs into a four- or five-week period where there are five or more days of volume distribution, or selling," says O'Neil. "This may sound new to most investors, but it is virtually impossible for the general market to go into an intermediate-term or bear market correction without this happening."

The indicator he uses primarily follows the actions of large institutions. He explains it in more detail: "We only count a distribution day when one of these indexes closes down two-tenths of a percent or more from the day before on heavier volume," he says, "and you can see an accumulation of five different days over a four- or five-week period. This historically has resulted in the market rolling over into a correction."

His indicator "is 80 to 90 percent accurate," O'Neil maintains. "It will take some time to learn what you're looking for, and the market indexes should be followed every day, because your 'raise cash' indication could evolve at any time or point." A count of the number of distribution days that have occurred day by day is displayed in the "Big Picture" column of *Investor's Business Daily*.

"These concepts serve as a helpful guideline to learning how to interpret the major indexes for yourself," O'Neil suggests. "People who spent the time to learn this system were able to sell and retreat into cash before major bear markets and protect a significant part of their prior period's earnings," he says. "And they avoided taking the excessive losses that many investors experienced in these difficult periods."

According to O'Neil's research, which contains a computer database covering 27 market cycles going back to 1880, "the highly successful market patterns have not changed. The main reason is because the law of supply and demand doesn't change, and neither does human nature."

O'Neil is not a big fan of most traditional technical indicators: "The concept of looking at a lot of indicators is a relatively mediocre method because nothing is as accurate as the market itself. The many indicators people use are derivatives, and many of them are based on theories and personal opinions about the basic items that you're trying to understand. Opinions are frequently wrong; markets seldom are."

ANALYZING INDIVIDUAL STOCKS

Nevertheless, O'Neil is a strong believer in using charts for both the market and individual stocks. When choosing individual stocks, he says that stocks go up based on 80 percent fundamentals such as which stock has an outstanding product that's gaining market share in its field. "You're looking for a company that's the current leader fundamentally as well as technically," he explains. "This can only be determined by daily, weekly, and monthly charts of the stock's price and volume action."

To be successful at picking stocks, O'Neil suggests that you "develop some ability at separating the very best companies fundamentally from all the other ones that don't measure up." He says, "You want to be able to see that the marketplace and the chart action are confirming what the fundamentals are showing.

To do this, you have to learn to read charts and seriously study patterns."

FINAL ADVICE

O'Neil has often told investors to create a set of rules before entering the market. "It's not enough to recognize which stocks to buy and when to buy them," he cautions. "You must also have a set of sell rules to nail down worthwhile gains once you have them, and even more important, a set of sell rules to cut short all mistakes."

In fact, O'Neil is famously known for telling investors to cut losses at 8 percent from the price they paid for the stock. "That's the only way to avoid 30 to 50 percent losses that can easily occur to any new or experienced investor," he says. "You can't sit with mistakes; you have to learn to read the market and listen to it, and not fight the reality of the market, which can be costly."

William J. O'Neil, at age 30 in the 1960s, became the youngest person at that time to buy a seat on the New York Stock Exchange. O'Neil was one of the first to use computers to analyze performance variables, and he pioneered landmark research that identified seven performance traits of the greatest market leaders before they make their biggest price gains. His research became the basis of the CAN SLIM Investment System. O'Neil launched *Investor's Business Daily* (*IBD*) in 1984, followed by the award-winning Web site, Investors.com. He is the author of numerous bestselling books, including the international classic *How to Make Money in Stocks: A Winning System in Good Times or Bad* (over 2 million copies sold). *Stock Trader's Almanac* dedicated its thirty-seventh edition to O'Neil.

WHAT'S NEXT?

The next chapter goes into more depth about the mysterious but game-changing use of high-frequency trading (HFT).

CHAPTER 9

High-Frequency Trading

Some of the old volume rules may not work as they once did. Perhaps the biggest change is the increasing use of algorithmic trading among computers, done at the speed of nanoseconds, primarily done at private hedge funds and trading desks at large banks. Insiders at these firms call these strategies "statistical arbitrage." Everyone else calls it *high-frequency trading*, or HFT.

You'll be hearing more about HFT as the U.S. Securities and Exchange Commission (SEC) and Congress try to understand exactly how these high-end, well-guarded strategies affect Wall Street.

Basically, computers are programmed to place millions of trades, playing havoc with volume, and then canceling them in seconds. Unfortunately, as a result of HFT, the reported volume that you see may not have the same meaning as it did in the past. Put another way, stock market volume statistics can be misleading.

If you are going to survive and thrive, you have to be flexible and adjust to the ever-evolving market. Reportedly, HFT volume has risen as high as 70 percent on some days. What does this mean to you? It means that looking only at the total day's volume is not necessarily a reliable indication of market strength. In addition, during the next market correction, computer-generated trades with preprogrammed algorithms could turn a correction into a severe crash.

To try and prevent future flash crashes, the SEC installed new "circuit-breaker" rules to halt or slow down trades if a stock moves

10 percent or more in a five-minute period. In addition, other proposals are being considered to further reduce these types of market disruptions. The goal, of course, is to make the market appear fair and orderly.

To better understand how high-frequency trading may affect Wall Street, I spoke with Shah Gilani, hedge fund manager and editor of WhatMovesMarkets.com. He's been studying HFT for a number of years.

Sincere: Is high-frequency trading adding liquidity to the markets?

Gilani: It's an illusion. The high-frequency guys can turn on their computers, and in a second's notice they can turn them off, and when they do, the perceived liquidity they provide in normally functioning markets dries up. We saw that in the "Flash Crash" in May 2010. Sometimes there isn't a lot of volume on either side of the quotes, so HFT takes advantage of that and pushes things up or down. For longer-term investors, and that means anything longer than a day trade, the ability to get into and out of positions when they need to is problematic. HFT is creating a false perception of liquidity. In reality, that is not what they are providing at all.

Sincere: Why is that a problem?

Gilani: First, volume is a principal indicator, and high-frequency trading skews the results. If you are not aware of the skew that it creates, you could be misled from any algorithms you create or any hypothesis you make. It could cause problems with your investing philosophy. It's estimated that on any given day over two-thirds of the volume comes from the rapid trading of HFT. So now that they are here, it could be a problem if they suddenly went away. Anyone who is looking for signs of normalcy in the markets needs to be concerned.

Sincere: What about the traditional volume indicators like On Balance Volume?

Gilani: I think they have to be viewed with some suspicion. HFT is not providing true liquidity as far as true commitment. The volume they provide is heavy because they are holding positions for a very short time, but no one really knows if they're holding for seconds or minutes. We assume they are closed out at the end of the day. So when you look at traditional volume indicators, you have no idea what you are looking at anymore. You look at some of the volume indicators and the volume you see is skewed.

Sincere: What should traders do?

Gilani: That's a great question, but right now I don't have the answer. As for me, I look at the big-picture volume and not individual stock volume. Now there is a lack of depth in the quotes, what bids and offers people are willing to line up and buy and sell for, and more importantly, how many shares are displayed in their quotes.

Sincere: When did the rules change?

Gilani: I believe that decimalization was the first mistake (when the bid and ask rules were changed from fractions to decimals). Decimalization gave an increased advantage to the specialists, market makers, and traders. Before decimalization, if a specialist wanted to step up ahead of an order, he had to risk an eighth. He'd have to pay twelve and a half cents for that risk. Now he can step ahead of an order and only risk a penny. As a result, specialists and market makers are taking more positions ahead of customer orders by stepping in front of them, which is advantageous for them because if their bet doesn't work out, they turn around and, for only a penny loss, dump their position for less risk. This has created more volatility, not because the spreads have narrowed but because the unintended consequence of narrowing spreads to reduce transaction costs for investors resulted in more trading opportunities for pros. Now, many investors are afraid to put down large orders because they may get slammed. So they're putting in 100 shares or 1,000 shares.

Sincere: How did HFT get so powerful?

Gilani: It started with the advent of public display electronic communication networks (ECNs), and the proliferation of private trading networks. Years ago, I thought that if someone could create a computer system that could bring all these disparate quotes from all the different trading venues together to get a "master quote," that person could game the system. And that's exactly what has happened. High-frequency traders have programmed their computers to track and trade off of all that information flow. They are getting all of the data from all these exchanges as fast as they can get it. It might have cost some of them $100 million to do it, but they can make that money back in less than a month.

Sincere: So it's all about reading order flow?

Gilani: Exactly. For some time, trading venues have been paying for order flow that once went to the big market makers and specialists. The more order flow, the more orders, and the more liquidity a venue can provide. It all adds up to more fees. But the advantage of order flow is you have the inside track. High-frequency traders now have an inside track into order flow and are using it to their advantage.

Sincere: Is HFT the root of all of these problems?

Gilani: Not completely. There are also the flash traders, who along with high-frequency traders, turned off their computers and helped cause the May 2010 Flash Crash. Flash traders are not always the same as high-frequency traders, though plenty of high-frequency traders use flash technology. Flash traders use a pinging methodology to determine the depth of the market. They are pinging around to all these venues looking for the best bid and offer and then actually putting down orders behind those bids and offers to see if they can attract more volume to the bids and offers ahead of them. They are using their computers to instantaneously probe order flow and to set up other computers to see what they want them to see, often to make them execute their orders. It happens so fast. Then they will pull their bids and offers within nanoseconds, either having executed an advantageous trade or leaving other traders holding the bag.

Sincere: Is that what happened during the 2010 Flash Crash?

Gilani: Exactly. In the Flash Crash, stocks went from $40, $60, or whatever, to basically $0. That never could have happened in the old days when the specialist and market makers were responsible for keeping fair and orderly markets. That would have been impossible. We're definitely in uncharted territory now. On the surface, high-frequency trades look like sound vehicles, but they are creating more noise disruptions than harmony.

Sincere: Who are the people behind HFT?

Gilani: They are mathematicians and computer scientists. It's the geeks first and traders second. They figured out how to trade on mathematical equations, essentially algorithms that are based on statistical arbitrage and quote and order flow arbitrage that have nothing to do with fundamentals like cash flows, earnings, and dividends. They only care about volume and the spread. They are quants who have programmed their computers to decipher mathematical relationships before anyone else can figure them out.

Sincere: Could these kinds of flash crashes happen again?

Gilani: They will try to put in triggers, but they won't stop it from happening again. We were lucky we got a glimpse of it. There were no bids during that hour. So the system, the NBBO [National Best Bid and Offer], was supposed to find a bid, but it couldn't find any bids? How is that possible? Now people are even afraid to put in a market stop-loss order because you could buy a stock at $50, put in a stop-loss order to sell it at $45, and discover a print went off at $30. You just sold your stock at $30. Before, in a horrible market, you might have gotten out with a half point loss. It's getting ridiculous. Many people have lost trust in the markets. They think the markets are rigged.

Sincere: Is there a solution?

Gilani: I have advocated for a national, centralized place for all of the bids and offers and all quotes from all venues to be centralized. There are ways for each venue to be compensated using a global book. That would be true liquidity. That would be a level playing field. It's nice to have competition among all these different venues but not when it affects the capital markets.

Sincere: Have you had to change the way you look at volume?

Gilani: Absolutely. I've been forced to use a number of strategies including arbitrage. Because it's become an HFT world, I'm spending a lot of time and money playing in their sandbox.

One of my strategies is looking at the spreads between the underlying stocks relative to the actual pricing of ETFs. It sounds complicated but it's really not. I have to do this because the other volume strategies aren't working. The cost to program this data runs into the millions of dollars. If I'm doing it, you can bet that teams of rocket scientists for all the big trading shops are also doing it. It's all wrong. The tail is wagging the dog. And the dog just happens to be the capital markets that make our economy.

Sincere: Thanks for sharing your insights.

Shah Gilani, a former Wall Street executive and hedge fund manager, runs a private equity firm from his base in Miami and is a contributing editor at MoneyMorning.com. He is also editor of the *Capital Wave Forecast* newsletter and owner of WhatMovesMarkets.com.

WHAT'S NEXT?

The creator of the next indicator, former software engineer Pascal Willain, developed a proprietary indicator to follow institutional volume. In the following interview, he gives an explanation of how he uses Effective Volume to gain an edge in the market.

CHAPTER 10

Effective Volume

Because Pascal Willain had a full-time job and was always late to the market, he developed his own price and volume indicator, Effective Volume (EV). (*Note:* A chart of Effective Volume is located in Chapter 12.)

So Willain quit his job several years ago and concentrated on perfecting his indicator, which reconstructs the original orders the institutions are sending to the market. Willain's statistical indicator, which he believes has also been developed by other financial institutions, determines if money is coming into or going out of the market.

"My goal at the beginning was to find out what the institutional players were doing at the transactional level," Willain says, "especially at critical points in a trend."

FOLLOW THE MONEY

Basically, his indicator follows where the big money is going by analyzing each market tick. "When institutions send orders to the market, they often hide them by dividing them into small orders," Willain says. So instead of seeing 10,000 shares, the computer often slices it into 100-share increments.

"I take all of the minute volume responsible for these minute price changes (Effective Volume), and separate them into two groups, large and small," Willain explains. "The large EV is what usually tells you what the institutional players are up to. I am measuring the interaction of price and volume, an interaction that occurs only when you have money moving in or out. You see everyone buy at one point or retract money at some point. So I'm measuring all of these spikes in the market, almost like a rocket launching."

By statistically sorting the minute-to-minute volume that provoked a price change, he can see the large player's money flow. "When the price changes from one minute to the next, it is usually the result of a change of equilibrium between buyers and sellers."

Where there is a big spike of money, he says, a new trend often starts, especially if money is flowing in for two days or more. "I can see the large volume orders so that tells me if institutions are buying or selling," says Willain. According to Willain, knowing what side of the market large players are on gives him an edge. He analyzes the data and posts the results on his Web site.

"It's important to see when the market changes so you can change your position," he says. "But once your position is changed, you keep it until the next big change," which could occur in a few weeks or months, he explains. Meanwhile, you would monitor your position.

Willain is careful to say that his indicator does not predict what the market does, but "it can give me a statistical advantage," he notes. "If a lot of large players are leaving the market, you can conclude the price will go down. I would simply follow the money because the money is always right."

He says his indicator usually gives an advance warning of two days of what might happen. "It's a balance between the buyers and sellers. But at a turning point the early sellers or early buyers will move first," observes Willain. It is at that critical point, before the trend changes, that Willain tries to catch the large players buying or selling.

VOLUME RULES

After price, volume is the most important piece of data. Willain notes: "You can trade price but you cannot trade volume. Volume can give you two pieces of information: the force of the move and the change in equilibrium, which can result in a trend change."

Willain explains the traditional way of looking at volume: A price move accompanied by increasing volume means that institutional players are participating in the move. In particular, buying a breakout on strong volume after a quiet period can be profitable. "The biggest problem with volume, however, is that it has no direction," Willain says. "It is mainly the direction of the price change that tells you if the volume is a buying or a selling volume."

According to Willain, the movement of a stock is "one-third determined by the market, one-third decided by the sector the stock is in, and one-third decided by the fundamentals of the company." So he begins his analysis by looking at the entire market, or top down.

"It's important to go from the big to the small picture," Willain says. "I first look at the total market. Then I determine if money is coming into or going out of the market. Once I have market direction, I study the different sectors. In each sector I have a money flow indicator that tells me if money is going in or out of the sector. I then buy stocks that are attracting the most money."

AIM FOR LESS RISK

Another way of studying volume is to look at the number of days the price goes up or down on increasing volume (distribution or accumulation days), which Willain also follows. "Short-term traders will usually buy the pullback, thinking the stock will continue on its uptrend, but mostly they wait for a breakout on strong volume," he says. "This is reliable, but I want to buy when money is moving in and no one notices."

He especially pays attention to pullbacks. "I look to see if there are a lot of institutional players entering a stock during pullbacks. I don't need to wait for the breakout because you never know when it will come. If a stock breaks out by 10 percent and you buy the breakout, you are basically buying the stock 10 percent higher. I want to buy when things are calm. Why should I lose 10 percent?" In case he is wrong, he puts his stop right below the closest price support level. "This way my risk is small," he adds.

Like any indicator, Effective Volume is not perfect. For example, sometimes the big money is wrong. To protect himself, he uses stops that cut his losses at 6 to 8 percent on the long side and 3 percent on the short side.

IGNORE PERSONAL OPINIONS

Like most disciplined traders, Willain has learned to ignore his personal opinions about the market. "If you listened to other people during a bear market, you'd be short all the time," he quips. "But that is not how the market moves. I don't want to trade my opinion. If the tools see money coming in, then money comes in, even if I believe otherwise. I follow my indicators."

One of the advantages of following his indicator is that he can ignore press releases and news reports that often lead investors in the wrong direction. "Often my indicator contradicts what is written in the press."

Sometimes an article comes out, he says, that will scare a lot of people into selling. "But Effective Volume is saying that large players are moving into the market."

More than likely, he follows his indicator.

Pascal Willain, formerly a mathematician and software engineer, lives in Brussels, Belgium, where he now trades full time. Before becoming a trader, he had created, managed, and sold a number of information technology companies. After retiring from his entrepreneurial activities, he started to invest his own funds in the market. Willain was fortunate enough to start this activity in 2001 when stock prices started to be calculated in cents ($0.01), which was the trigger for the stating of high-frequency trading algorithms. He discovered several groundbreaking trading algorithms that he has detailed in his book *Value in Time: Better Trading through Effective Volume* (Wiley, 2008). Willain's indicators are published each day on the www.effectivevolume.com Web site.

Buying Power Index

Lowry Research Corp., the oldest technical advisory firm in the United States, uses a proprietary volume indicator, Buying Power Index, to analyze market conditions. Although the buying and selling pressure formula is a closely held secret, Lowry routinely publishes the results for individuals and institutions.

Back in the 1930s when Lowry first developed the formula, it calculated the results by hand. Points were assigned for whether volume was up or down for the day. "It's almost an early form of the NYSE TICK data," explains Richard Dickson, Lowry's senior market strategist and market commentator. "We are counting points gained or lost for all the stocks on the exchange each day. The difference is that it's done on a cumulative basis and not tick by tick."

If you had to summarize the trading philosophy of Lowry, it follows the trend. "A trend in motion tends to stay in motion until you see something that says it's going to reverse," Dickson says. "We don't try to predict when it is going to stop."

Lowry constantly analyzes the various stages of the trend carefully for any signs it could stop, also studying historical and current market conditions.

In March 2009, Lowry got a 96 Buying Power Index (BPI) reading at the bear market bottom, one of the lowest readings ever recorded. "Buying power got so low we wondered if it was going to drop below zero," Dickson jests.

At first, they questioned whether the numbers had been warped by hedge funds exiting the market. After analyzing the data, Lowry concluded that the evidence favored the bull side. They put out an intermediate buy alert in August 2009, which turned out to be correct, although not the precise bottom.

If there is a secret to using indicators, Dickson says it's to know their nuances: "Not every indicator works all the time. You have to understand when it works and when it doesn't. The worst thing you can do is to be on a search for that secret ingredient that will tell you what the market will do. You end up like a dog chasing its tail."

How does he know when his indicators stop working? "That's easy," he quips. "You're losing money." He is sometimes surprised that indicators he has depended on in the past suddenly stop working.

"Indicators stop working when the character of the market stops working," Dickson explains. "A classic example is the 'odd lot' trading indicator, which used to be a sentiment indicator. The options market and electronic exchanges made the odd lot indicator obsolete."

Because the market environment constantly changes, Dickson routinely evaluates his indicators. Nevertheless, he warns, "I have learned over the years that ignoring your indicators is at your own peril. What invariably happens is that the indicators were right but its reactions might be delayed."

"My advice to people is to be a student of the market," Dickson says, "and that means learning as much as possible. The market is always right, and you can only be wrong. You have to be humble and flexible and be willing to take losses, especially if you are trading. The biggest mistake is the refusal to take a loss."

WHAT'S NEXT?

In Part Four, which should be extremely useful, you'll find out where to go for help if you want to learn more about indicators. For now, many of you will find the next piece in Chapter 11, "What to Do in a Market Emergency," required reading.

One Step Beyond

The information in the following chapters should help you decide what to do before the next market emergency. In addition, you'll find a list of important resources, including a glossary, an indicator "cheat sheet," useful charts, and where to go if you want to take indicators to a higher level. When time is *not* on your side, these chapters could be portfolio savers.

CHAPTER 11

Timely Advice

Now that I've talked to the experts, conducted the research, and traded using market indicators, I'd like to share a few observations with you. You may or may not agree with my conclusions, but keep in mind these are my opinions. I'll begin by giving you a few suggestions in case you are confronted with a market emergency.

WHAT TO DO IN A MARKET EMERGENCY

If you are reading this for entertainment and it's not a market emergency, take steps now to prepare for worst-case scenarios. Obviously, the best time to make financial decisions is when you *want* to, not when you *have* to. In the stock market, anything can happen, so it's best to prepare before you are caught by surprise.

If, however, this is a real market emergency, and you're nervous or scared, read the next section. It may help keep you calm.

Surviving Market Meltdowns

It never fails. When you are feeling the most emotional, confused, and vulnerable, you'll read a series of articles about how the market will completely collapse tomorrow. Perhaps you'll get a call from a panicked friend who tells you to "sell everything now!"

To survive market crashes and corrections, you must keep your head while others are losing theirs (to paraphrase Rudyard Kipling). As I said before, the stock market is a psychological battlefield that can cause extreme emotions ranging from fear to greed.

One thing I know for sure: The worst time to make financial decisions is when you're overly emotional. Before you make an impulsive decision, confirm what you think will happen with the indicators included in this book. More than likely, some of the indicators will be off the charts.

When the market is impersonating a falling knife, people always try to guess the bottom. How low can it go? Trying to predict the bottom (or the top, for that matter) can be frustratingly difficult.

If you're an investor, you may be interested in what Peter Lynch, bestselling author and legendary Fidelity mutual fund manager, told me. When I asked him if it's possible to predict the market, he replied: "I've been trying to get next year's *Wall Street Journal* for 40 years. I'd pay an extra dollar for it. I'd love to know what will happen in the future. I have no idea what the market will do over the next one or two years. What I do know is that if interest rates go up, inflation will go up and the stock market will go down. I also know that historically, about once every two years the market has a decline of between 10 and 20 percent. These are called corrections. Perhaps one out of three of these corrections will turn into a decline of 20 percent or greater. These are called 'bear markets.' If you understand what you own, you're in good shape. If you don't know what you own, and don't understand what a company does and it falls in half, what do you do? Call the psychic hotline? If you understand clearly what the company does and you understand who the competitors are, and the market goes down and the stock goes down, you don't panic."

If you're a trader, you also don't panic. Force yourself not to make any irrational trades. Turn off the computer, get some exercise, or take a drive. Read *Reminiscences of a Stock Operator* for commonsense advice. The following passage from the book is particularly helpful: "Obviously the thing to do was to be bullish in a bull market and bearish in a bear market. Sounds silly, doesn't it? But I had to grasp that general principle firmly before I saw that to put it into practice really meant to anticipate probabilities. It took me a long time to learn to trade on those lines."

If you have time, watch the movie *Wall Street* (1987), or its sequel (2010), for more lessons. Don't forget that doing the opposite of the crowd is often the right move, especially at extremes. Also, remember that the market goes up more than it goes down.

If you have any doubts about your position, take a small loss now before it turns into a more painful loss later. Often the market gives you a second chance to get out. Sell while you still can. Let your winners keep winning. Sometimes you have to grit your teeth and wait, doing the opposite of what you feel. Other times you have to take immediate action.

I hope this helps. Good luck and stay calm.

WHAT I REALLY THINK OF MARKET INDICATORS

The purpose of this book is to help you learn all about market indicators. Nevertheless, I have left one question unanswered: Can indicators really predict what the market will do next?

Searching for a Silver Bullet

I am certain of this: by using indicators, you can increase the probabilities that a particular trade or investment will be profitable. For this reason alone, you need to use market indicators. But using indicators to make market forecasts is not as clear-cut.

Unfortunately, no one has been able to consistently predict the market's highs or lows, and also attach a date to it. The ones who have been right about market direction are usually careful to say they don't know exactly when it will happen.

Nevertheless, many have searched in vain for an indicator that can make accurate predictions, but so far it has remained elusive. The Holy Grail, as the pros call it, is the dream of anyone who creates market indicators. Many are still searching.

At the same time, don't listen to people who try to sell you on the idea they have a magic indicator. If they really had such an indicator, they wouldn't share it with you or give you any of the imaginary profits.

More Art Than Science

In my opinion, market indicators are the Global Positioning System (GPS) you use in your car. A GPS can lead you in the right direction, but in the end, you have to use your own judgment. If you follow GPS too literally, you might end up in the ditch. This system wasn't designed to drive your car, and market indicators aren't designed to make trades for you. Indicators are trustworthy tools that provide important information and clues, but to make any money, you must connect the dots.

You can also use market indicators to keep your emotions in check. Sadly, because most people are so emotional, they often make terrible trading decisions. If the indicator says the market is going down but you think it is going up, more than likely you'd do well to follow the indicator. Keeping you emotionless is the main reason indicators are so valuable.

Although indicators aren't perfect, they still provide you with enough clues and advance warning to make them so essential. Some people will ask you how much money you would have lost if you had missed the 10 best days in the market. Yes, you would have lost out on the opportunity to make more money. Then again, how much would you have saved if you had missed the 10 *worst* days? Using indicators can help you avoid those kinds of days.

Indicatoritis and Other Problems

Although indicators are just tools and not a silver bullet, some people misuse them. Perhaps the most common problem is using indicators to reinforce your current beliefs about the market. If you want, you can make an indicator "confess to anything," as Bernard Baumohl put it. Let the indicator tell you where to go, rather than vice versa.

Another common mistake is using too many indicators at one time. This is a condition known as "Indicatoritis," as blog commenter Treeshaker jokingly called it. He went on to write, "You might have a case of Indicatoritis, which is a severe inflammation of your chart indicator glands. This invariably leads to analysis paralysis, the complete and utter inability to pull the trigger and trade at all."

To really become proficient with indicators, as the experts point out, you need to practice, practice, practice. Play around with the default settings, switch time periods, use the indicators in many different market environments, and test them out on individual stocks.

What Have You Done for Me Lately?

It's easy for anyone to look back on a chart and give examples of how you could have, should have, or would have made a fortune if you had entered the market when line Y crossed line Z. The challenging part is using the indicators to make a trade now.

If you are looking for a 100 percent, risk-free guaranteed trade, keep looking and good luck. However, if you are willing to trade or invest based on probabilities, then indicators can help. But don't get me wrong: if you hand a mediocre trader the best indicator in the world, he or she may still make mediocre trades.

Why? It's like giving a mediocre golfer the most expensive golf club ever created. It will probably improve his game, but he still won't make it to the Masters Golf Tournament. Therefore, indicators can give you market insights and can also improve your trading, but to consistently make money you need to develop all of your skills.

Finally, take the time to listen to the market. If you really listen, you can't help but be on the only side that counts: the right side.

WHAT'S NEXT?

Thomas DeMark, bestselling author and creator of several well-known indicators, stopped by to share his thoughts on using market indicators. He's had an illustrious career working with fund managers using his proprietary market-timing services.

THOMAS DEMARK: CREATOR, TD SEQUENTIAL AND TD COMBO

THE ANTITREND INDICATOR

Thomas DeMark is well known in the trading community for creating a series of indicators with his trademark name. Using an old Texas Instrument calculator, he dreamed up his first indicator after studying charts and subscribing to various chart services.

"Everything was done by chart comparisons and charts I did myself as well as using a magnifying glass. It took a lot of time."

Ironically, although he constructed technical indicators, DeMark no longer considers himself a technician. "I'm sort of a hybrid. I think fundamentals dictate long-term trends. I also think that a fundamentalist has to use market timing."

From that inauspicious start, he is part of an ongoing research team that develops various indicators, including TD Sequential and TD Combo, the nucleus of all his indicators. (*Note:* A chart of TD Sequential is located in Chapter 12.)

"My approach is different from other people's because I was raised on the institutional side of the market," DeMark says. "At that time, we didn't want to be like everyone else, which was trend following. So we had to anticipate tops and bottoms. Most of the indicators we developed are anticipatory. They're antitrend, but at opportune times."

Opportune for DeMark includes recognizing the inflection points when the trend is going to change, usually at market extremes. "We try to anticipate the trend," he explains. "On the downside, it's like trying to catch a falling knife. You can get hurt."

As a market goes higher and higher, he says, his indicators get progressively more bearish. As a market extends into the future, you'll see fewer and fewer stocks making new highs. "That's when we look for a divergence in price," he says. "We'll also look at indicators such as New High–New Low. We also look at the components of an index and compare it against its price move."

One of the problems with trend following, DeMark says, is that you usually come in 20 percent late off the low and sell 20 percent early off the high. "Markets typically operate in trading ranges," he points out. "They move sideways over an extended period of time. Any stock is in a trading range 76 to 82 percent of the time. Of that remaining 18 to 24 percent, about 12 to 14 percent of the markets trend up. Of the difference, about 6 percent of the markets trend down. Why do markets trend up longer than markets trend down? Because buying is an accumulative process and analysts become more positive as the market goes higher. As the market rallies, people become more positive and margin accounts are added. People's conviction is reinforced as the market rallies. It's a cumulative decision to buy."

On the other hand, he says, when people don't like something, they make one quick decision to sell. "And that's why declines are a lot sharper than advances," he explains. "It's just one decision to sell, whereas buying occurs in increments."

When you follow the trend, DeMark points out, it doesn't matter which moving average indicator you use: they will all work, and so will any trend-following indicator. But when a market is in a trading range—a more challenging market—you have to turn to oscillators, especially those that can tell you when the market will break out or reverse.

During those times, DeMark attempts to identify divergences, which he says work when the market is in a trading range. "The reason market oscillators conform to divergences sometimes, not all the time, is because of duration, the amount of time which an indicator resides in an overbought or oversold condition. If it's overbought for more than seven bars, then you are extremely overbought. If you're there for less than seven bars, you are mildly overbought. The market will top when you are mildly overbought or oversold. If you are extremely overbought or oversold, the markets are in a trend, and you're smarter not to do anything or go with the flow of the trend."

He also measures supply and demand. "Supply and demand drives the market, so we try and measure when supply and demand are exhausted. If the market exhausts itself, typically the market will go sideways. The internal aspects of the market will forewarn us that it is just a respite or decline."

And when markets rally, DeMark says, it's not because of smart buyers at the bottom but because the last seller has sold. "And conversely, highs are not made because of smart sellers but because the last buyer has bought."

THE CREATIVE USE OF INDICATORS

DeMark explains there are three levels of chart analysis, which is what most technical indicators are based on.

"The first level I call chartists, or chart artists," DeMark says. "They try to predict the future based on a chart without tools. Their biases and predispositions dictate what their conclusions are."

The next level, he says, are indicators: "With indicators, you formulate conclusions based on history, time periods, and ideal price points."

"The third level is the systematic approach," DeMark explains, "taking the indicators and systemizing them."

DeMark says he operates on the second level, creating proprietary indicators. Although he could systemize his indicators, he's chosen not to, primarily because it doesn't allow him as much creativity.

One of the things that DeMark does with indicators is to view time periods uniquely. "We don't use terminology such as *long*, *short*, and *intermediate* the way most people do," he explains. "For most people, they will say that short-term is two weeks. We use it in context of return. We might say that short-term is a 10 percent move. An intermediate term is a 25 percent move, and anything over 25 percent is a long-term move. We could accomplish what some people perceive as a two-week return in an hour and then be out of our position."

SEARCHING FOR THE MARKET'S HOLY GRAIL

Unlike some, DeMark has no qualms about his goal: using market-timing indicators to predict the market. "There are times when we've been so precise it will boggle your mind," he says. "But there are also times when we are wrong."

DeMark freely admits his life's ambition is to find the market's Holy Grail, which means the elusive but perfect indicator that can predict where the market will go next. "We're looking for the Holy Grail, and eventually I'm going to find it. We've found some things that are very accurate, but it's about getting everything into a computer and making it automatic."

DeMark's closing advice: "While a trading strategy is critical, more important are trading discipline and money management skills. Without these two important elements, a trader is destined to failure."

Tom DeMark has been involved in the investment business for over 40 years. Upon graduation with a B.A. and MBA and after law school, DeMark went to work for one of the fastest-growing investment counseling firms. He became president of a consulting subsidiary that sold market-timing services to many of the largest and most successful funds and trusts in the country. For the past 17 years DeMark has been special advisor to Steve Cohen, principal of SAC Capital. DeMark is also president of Market Studies LLC, a supplier of market-timing services to Bloomberg, Thomson Reuters, CQG, and, recently, DeMark Prime. DeMark has written three bestselling books and is a speaker at many worldwide investment forums and seminars. Additionally, he regularly appears on financial networks.

WHAT'S NEXT?

In the next chapter, I'll provide you with lots of useful resources including where to get help, an indicator summary, charts, books, and stock discussion groups.

CHAPTER 12

Where to Get Help

If you are going to participate in the financial markets, become a student. Read books, study, and analyze. Don't rely on others to do all of the homework for you. Understanding the stock market can be a lifelong pursuit, and to succeed you need a continuous education. This book is one small step. The next step is yours. For now, here are some useful resources and ideas for further study.

THE HELP DESK

As mentioned earlier, if you have questions about market indicators while reading this book, call the Help Desk at your brokerage firm. As long as you're a customer, the professionals at your brokerage firm should answer your questions. (You can also send me an e-mail, if you want.) Finally, if you'd like to study indicators on your own, the following is a list of some very helpful resources.

BOOKS FOR EMERGING TRADERS AND INVESTORS

The books below should help you expand your knowledge about the stock market, including learning more about market indicators:

Technical Analysis Plain and Simple (FT Press, 3rd edition, 2010), by Michael Kahn: An easy-to-read introduction to technical analysis and market indicators.

How to Make Money in Stocks (McGraw-Hill, 4th edition, 2009), by
   William J. O'Neil: This bestseller shows investors how to profit
   in the market by using a rule-based, systematic approach.

The Visual Investor: How to Spot Market Trends (Wiley, 2009), by
   John J. Murphy: A thoughtful introduction to technical analysis
   and the nuances of using market indicators.

*Market Indicators: The Best-Kept Secret to More Effective Trading and
   Investing* (Bloomberg, 2009), by Richard Sipley: An
   understandable and well-researched book for helping long-
   term investors use market indicators.

A Beginner's Guide to Short-Term Trading (Adams Media, 2008), by
   Toni Turner: An easy-to-read bestseller aimed at novice traders
   about short-term trading tactics and tools, including market
   indicators.

Market Wizards (Marketplace Books, classic edition, 2006) and *The
   New Market Wizards* (Marketplace Books, 2008), by Jack
   Schwager: The author delves into the minds of successful
   traders in these two classics.

The Secrets of Economic Indicators (Wharton, 2007), by Bernard
   Baumohl: A detailed but easy-to-read guide to helping
   investors use and interpret economic indicators.

Reminiscences of a Stock Operator (Wiley, revised edition, 2006), by
   Edwin Lefèvre: A must-read classic about the trading
   adventures of legendary trader Jesse Livermore. This book is
   as relevant today as it was in the early 1920s.

When Genius Failed (Random House, 2001), by Roger Lowenstein:
   Bestseller about the rise and fall of Long-Term Capital
   Management, a hedge fund run by some of the smartest
   people in the country.

Extraordinary Popular Delusions and the Madness of Crowds (Wiley,
   1995), by Charles MacKay: This classic, originally written in
   the nineteenth century, proves that human behavior never
   seems to change, which makes this book so valuable.

Trading for a Living (Wiley, 1993), by Alexander Elder: A
   bestselling book on the psychological challenges of the market
   as well as how to use market indicators when trading.

Stock Trader's Almanac (Wiley), by Jeffrey A. Hirsch and Yale Hirsch: A popular yearly almanac loaded with calendar-based indicators, including graphs, historical charts, market data, and economic events.

BOOKS FOR EXPERIENCED TRADERS

The authors of the following books explore trading and market indicators in more detail:

Trading with the VIX (Wiley, 2011), by Bill Luby

DeMark Indicators (Bloomberg, 2008), by Jason Perl

Value in Time: Better Trading through Effective Volume (Wiley, 2008), by Pascal Willain

The Secret Science of Price and Volume (Wiley, 2008), by Tim Ord

Trade Your Way to Financial Freedom (McGraw-Hill, 2006), by Van K. Tharp

Candlestick Charting Explained (McGraw-Hill, 2006), by Gregory Morris

Technical Analysis: Power Tools for Active Investors (FT Press, 2005), by Gerald Appel

The Complete Guide to Market Breadth Indicators (McGraw-Hill, 2005), by Gregory Morris

The Encyclopedia of Technical Market Indicators (McGraw-Hill, 2003), by Robert Colby

Technical Analysis Explained (McGraw-Hill, 2002), by Martin J. Pring

Bollinger on Bollinger Bands (McGraw-Hill, 2001), by John Bollinger

Japanese Candlestick Charting Techniques (Prentice Hall, 2001), by Steve Nison

Technical Analysis from A to Z (McGraw-Hill, 2000), by Steven B. Achelis

The Master Swing Trader (McGraw-Hill, 2000), by Alan Farley

Technical Analysis of the Financial Markets (NY Institute of Finance, 1999), by John J. Murphy

Long-Term Secrets for Short-Term Trading (Wiley, 1999), by Larry Williams

Technical Analysis for the Trading Professional (McGraw-Hill, 1999),
   by Constance Brown
The Arms Index (TRIN Index) (Marketplace Books, 1996), by
   Richard Arms
Street Smarts: High Probability Short-Term Trading Strategies (M.
   Gordon Publishing, 1996), by Linda Raschke
New Concepts in Technical Trading Systems (1978), by Welles Wilder

WEB SITES THAT INCLUDE MARKET INDICATORS

www.stockcharts.com: StockCharts.com is designed to inform
   you about all aspects of technical indicators. Check out the
   "Chart School" tab for a broad education on how to use
   various indicators. It also has an informative blog that uses
   various indicators to analyze the stock market. If you're
   passionate about market indicators, this is the place to visit.

www.market-harmonics.com: The Market Harmonics Web site
   contains charts of numerous sentiment surveys, including
   Investors Intelligence, Consumer Confidence survey, the CBOE
   Put/Call Ratio, and Volatility studies. Click on the "Market
   Momentum" link on the home page.

www.barchart.com: Barchart was one of the earliest Web sites
   devoted to helping traders use charts. Check out the Learning
   Center, which contains a tutorial on technical indicators.

www.decisionpoint.com: Decision Point is designed to help
   traders use technical indicators. Check out the "Learning
   Center" tab for an indicator education. A number of
   experienced technicians visit this site.

www.bigcharts.com: Bigcharts is an interactive chart program
   that includes market indicators.

www.investopedia.com: Investopedia is loaded with definitions
   and explanations of market indicators as well as anything
   connected to the stock market. This site is aimed at the novice
   investor and trader.

www.wsj.com: The *Wall Street Journal* online and the daily print
   edition contain key stock market information and news for
   traders and investors. Check out the online Market Data

Center, which displays the results of numerous indicators. Click on the words "Market Data" from the front page.

www.barrons.com: *Barron's* online and the weekly print edition contain the same key stock market information for traders and investors as the *Wall Street Journal*. Check out its online Market Data Center, which displays the results of numerous indicators. Click on the title "Market Data" from the drop-down menu on the home page.

www.investors.com: *Investor's Business Daily* online and the daily print edition contain key stock market information and breaking news for traders and investors. Check out "Market Pulse" on *IBD's* home page, which gives a summary of its proprietary indicators.

www.ft.com: *Financial Times*, based in the United Kingdom, contains key stock market information and breaking news for traders and investors, but with a European perspective.

www.forbes.com: *Forbes* magazine's online and print edition contain financial news, analysis, and insights into the stock market.

www.google.com/finance: Google Finance contains chart software, breaking news stories, and stock quotes. You can also do a Google news search using the term *market indicator*.

finance.yahoo.com: Yahoo! Finance contains chart software, breaking news stories, and stock quotes. Check out its "Market Stats" page under the "Investing" tab, which displays the results of many indicators. You can also do a Yahoo! news search using the term *market indicator*.

www.cnbc.com: CNBC has an online site that contains breaking financial news and commentary. Check out the "Markets" tab on its home page for indicator results. If you want more information, CNBC provides continuous television and radio coverage of stock market news and commentary during the day.

www.bloomberg.com: *Bloomberg* updates breaking financial news on its Web site, which also includes economic calendars and some basic information for nonsubscribers. Bloomberg also provides continuous television and radio coverage of stock market news and commentary during the day.

www.smartmoney.com: *Smart Money* online and the print edition contain financial news, commentary, and insights into the stock market.

www.kiplinger.com: *Kiplinger* online and the print edition contain financial news, commentary, and insights into the stock market.

money.cnn.com: *Money* magazine online and the print edition contain financial news, commentary, and insights into the stock market.

www.activetrademag.com: *Active Trader*'s monthly online magazine is geared to traders, and it often includes in-depth interviews and analysis of market indicators.

www.marketwatch.com: MarketWatch contains breaking news and articles about the stock market, including lots of commentaries from independent sources. Check out the Front Page, which often includes an analysis of market indicators such as investment advisory newsletters.

www.briefing.com: Briefing provides independent analysis and commentary, trading ideas, and research tools for traders and investors.

www.schaeffersresearch.com: Schaeffer's Investment Research contains articles and commentary on market indicators as well as stock and options market information.

www.aaii.com: The American Association of Individual Investors Web site contains the AAII sentiment survey.

www.investorsintelligence.com: The Investors Intelligence Web site contains the Advisor Sentiment Survey.

www.cboe.com: The CBOE Web site primarily contains options educational material, including CBOE Put/Call Ratios and the VIX.

www.ise.com: The International Securities Exchange Web site primarily contains options data, including ISEE Call/Put Ratios.

www.seekingalpha.com: The Seeking Alpha blog contains breaking news, articles, and investment ideas aimed at traders and investors, including many articles on using market indicators.

www.thekirkreport.com: Charles Kirk, creator of The Kirk Report, searches for key stock market information, including market indicators, and displays it on his popular Web site as a link.

www.tradersnarrative.com: The Trader's Narrative blog often contains commentary and analysis of market indicators, especially sentiment indicators.

www.indexindicators.com: Index Indicators displays over 450 market indicators, including numerous stock indexes from other countries.

www.moneyshow.com and **www.tradersexpo.com:** The Money Show and Traders Expo are popular trade shows packed with trading and investing superstars. The Money Show Web site also contains investment advice.

STOCK DISCUSSION GROUPS

You can also look for trader forums at your brokerage firm. If you are unsure where to look, use a search engine to find discussion groups, including a few of the most well-known stock groups, below:

messages.yahoo.com (Yahoo!)

groups.google.com (Google)

www.ragingbull.com (Raging Bull)

www.investors.com (*IBD* Community)

www.traders-talk.com (Traders-Talk)

www.trade2win.com (Trade 2 Win)

www.elitetrader.com (Elite Trader)

groups.google.com/group/marketslist (Markets List)

www.investorvillage.com (Investor Village)

www.siliconinvestor.com (Silicon Investor)

value-in-time@googlegroups.com (Effective Volume)

Backtesting Ideas

With the help of a trading friend, we conducted an independent backtest of the five technical indicators in Chapter 3 using Fidelity Investment's Wealth Lab Pro.

Why should you backtest? First, backtesting allows you to test your trading ideas and indicators, playing "what if" games with the results, and changing time periods and rules. Backtesting is a powerful and flexible tool that can also be a fund saver.

For example, several years ago, an investment bank backtested Bernard Madoff's Ponzi-scheme trading strategy, but it couldn't match his results. This blaring red flag convinced the bank to invest its money elsewhere, saving its client's portfolio.

Obviously, backtesting is not 100 percent foolproof. Sometimes the profits seem almost too good to be true, but when you try to duplicate the results in real life, you end up making far less, and perhaps even lose money.

For example, backtesting doesn't include false or misleading signals, which adversely affects results. And backtesting assumes no human interference, which is probably not realistic for most retail traders. Also, just because these indicators worked in the past doesn't guarantee they will work in the future—conditions may change.

I had my trader friend choose a really wild three-year period, when the market crashed one year, but came roaring back the following year (2007 to 2010). For our simulation, we included all of the stocks in the S&P 500, assuming $5,000 to buy or sell each stock. We also compared the indicators with a buy-and-hold strategy, buying every stock in the S&P 500 one time ($5,000 x 500), and holding.

Because of time limitations, my trader friend couldn't do the kind of precise, detailed testing that professional traders and statisticians require. This was simply a first-run test to give us an idea of how indicators performed during a random three-year period. Based on the results of the backtest, I learned that no one should favor one indicator over another. If anything, these tests show the power and potential of backtesting.

What did I discover? First, most backtest programs have preprogrammed strategies built into the software. For example, you could quickly run tests on the moving average crossover strategy for any time period. You can also run tests on many other popular strategies. When my friend generated the test on the indicators, he didn't include stop losses, so the results were a bit skewed. Although all of the indicators resulted in huge gains, the category "Maximum Drawdown" was rather interesting. Maximum Drawdown refers to the point where you had your worst losses. In the depths of a market crash, almost all of the indicators had rather large drawdowns. My trading friend explained that because we didn't use stop losses, this was to be expected.

When most people look at the results of a backtest, they immediately look at the "Net Profit" category. And if you saw the final results of our indicator backtest, you'd be impressed. But the pros might be more interested in Maximum Drawdown, because to them, large drawdowns are unacceptable.

There was another tidbit: every single indicator beat the buy-and-hold strategy over the three-year period. Not surprisingly, however, during the last year of the test, when the market went up almost 70 percent in a year, buy-and-hold did just as well as the indicators.

In addition to not using stop losses, it took some time to agree on the rules. Moving Averages were simple: When the 20-day crossed over the 50-day, we bought. When the 20-day crossed below the 50-day, we sold. It was also easy to create rules for MACD: When MACD crossed above the zero line, we bought. When MACD crossed below the zero line, we sold.

But the rules for RSI, Stochastics, and Bollinger Bands were not as clear. Just to experiment, we bought when RSI crossed below 30 and sold when it crossed above 70. For Stochastics, we used 20 and 80, although we were aware these were not designed to be actionable trades.

In case you were curious, Bollinger Bands had the best results, which was probably because the three-year period was so volatile and Bollinger Bands self-adapt in this type of environment and automatically widen when volatility increases. RSI and Moving Averages were nearly tied for second place with huge profits.

I considered publishing the results of the backtests but didn't think it was fair to include a first-run test. Now that the data has been entered into the backtest program, we can continue experimenting. Although past results cannot guarantee future profits, testing helps to determine which indicators are best suited for the current, and future, market environment.

CHARTS

The following are additional charts of technical indicators discussed in the book.

FIGURE 12.1

MACD (Moving Average Convergence Divergence)

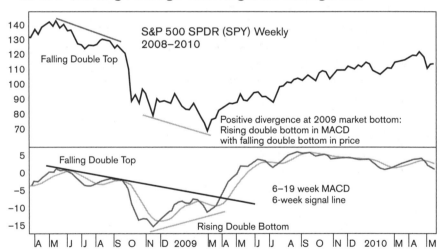

Source: Gerald Appel

FIGURE 12.2

SQN (System Quality Number)

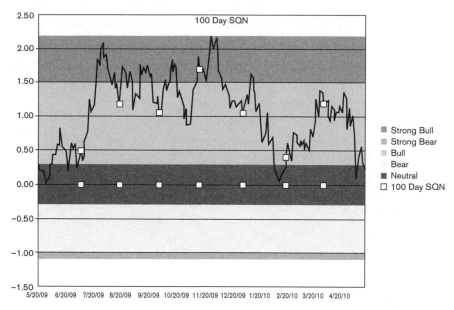

Source: Dr. Van Tharp

Comment: The SQN for the S&P 500 through May 17, 2010. Notice that while the reading is still neutral, it looks quite ominous in a chart form.

FIGURE 12.3

Williams %R

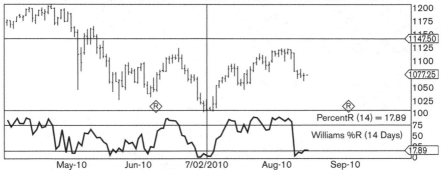

ES-067: 09/09/1997 – 08/17/2010 (Daily bars) E-Mini S&P 500 Cad Liq – Template: Default
Fri 07/02/2010 (ES-201009): O = 1022.45 H = 1032.50 L = 1010.75 C = 1014.25 TdofM = 2 TdofY = 130

Source: Larry Williams

FIGURE 12.4

TD Sequential

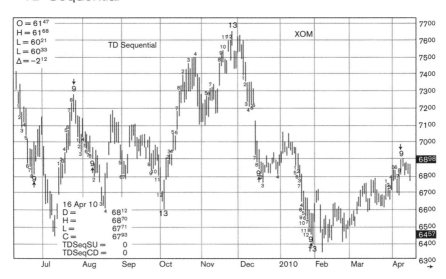

Source: Thomas DeMark. CQG Inc., copyright 2010, all rights reserved worldwide (www.cqg.com).

FIGURE 12.5

Distribution Days

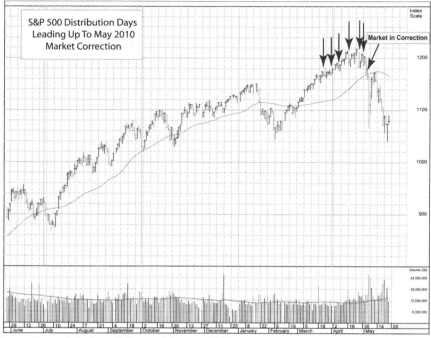

S&P 500 Distribution Days Leading Up To May 2010 Market Correction

Market in Correction

Source: *Investor's Business Daily*, copyright 2010, all rights reserved.

FIGURE 12.6

Force Index

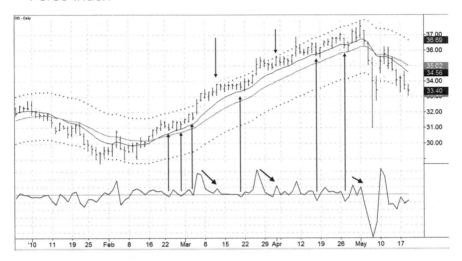

Force Index Source: Alexander Elder

Comment: This chart of Disney illustrates that when the trend is up and a short-term Force Index dips below its centerline, it gives a buy signal. Its bearish divergences, marked by diagonal arrows, provide sell signals.

FIGURE 12.7

Effective Volume

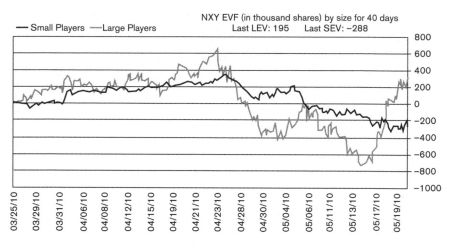

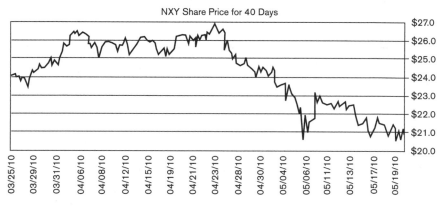

Source: Pascal Willain

Comment: The first figure represents the buying power that is pushing NXY to reverse. The second figure compares the money flow of different stocks within one sector. We can see that NXY stands out compared to the others (MF = EV × Price).

FIGURE 12.8

FIGURE 12.8

Bollinger Bands

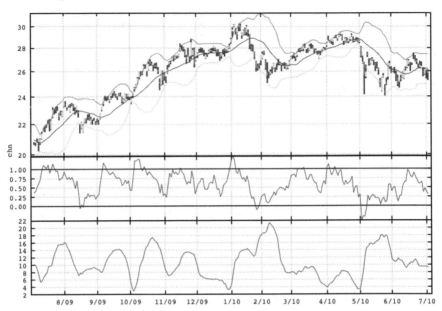

Source: Courtesy of Bollinger Capital (www.BollingerBands.com).

GLOSSARY: MORE POPULAR
TECHNICAL INDICATORS

Although there are hundreds of technical indicators, the following is a brief list of definitions of the most common indicators found on many brokerage firms' software.

Accumulation Distribution: The Accumulation Distribution Line is a cumulative indicator that evaluates how much money is flowing into and out of a stock.

Average Directional Index (ADX): The Average Directional Index determines the strength of the current trend.

Average True Range: The Average True Range measures the volatility of an individual stock.

Bollinger Band Width: This indicator is one of two indicators (the other is %B) that can be derived from Bollinger Bands.

Bollinger Bands: Bollinger Bands measure volatility expansions and contractions using bands that are set two standard deviations above and below the 20-day moving average.

CBOE Nasdaq Market Volatility (VXN): The VXN measures the volatility of the market as conveyed by the implied volatility of Nasdaq 100 index option prices.

CBOE Volatility Index (VIX): The VIX measures the volatility of the market as conveyed by the implied volatility of S&P 500 stock index options.

Chaikin Money Flow: This indicator is used to determine if individual stocks are experiencing accumulation (buying) or distribution (selling) pressure.

Chande Momentum Oscillator: This oscillator determines if a stock is overbought or oversold.

Commodity Channel Index: Another oscillator, the Commodity Channel Index is used to determine if a stock is overbought or oversold, in addition to identifying cyclical turns in commodities.

Exponential Moving Average: This moving average gives greater weight to the most recent closing prices.

Keltner Channel: An envelope indicator with a fixed band, the Keltner Channel measures stock movements.

MACD (Moving Average Convergence Divergence): This is a momentum indicator that shows the relationship between two moving averages, which can help determine entries or exits.

McClellan Oscillator: This is a momentum oscillator of net advances (advances less declines). It gives more information about the Advance-Decline Line statistics and measures the acceleration that occurs in the market breadth numbers.

McClellan Summation Index: This breadth indicator identifies the market's current trend.

Money Flow Index (MFI): This is a momentum indicator that measures the strength of money flowing into and out of a stock, either positive or negative.

Moving Average Envelope: This indicator, surrounded by two other moving averages (envelope), is designed to identify trend changes.

Negative Volume Index: This index analyzes volume decreases from the previous day.

NYSE TICK: Used primarily by intraday traders, the NYSE TICK monitors short-term overbought or oversold conditions.

NYSE TRIN (Arms Index): The Arms Index is a breadth indicator that identifies overbought or oversold conditions.

On Balance Volume (OBV): OBV is a momentum indicator that analyzes volume flow into and out of individual stocks.

Parabolic SAR: This is used to set trailing price stops for short or long positions, depending on the direction of the trend.

Positive Volume Index (PVI): This indicator zeroes in on the days when volume has increased from the previous day.

Price/Earnings (P/E) Ratio: The granddaddy of fundamental indicators, the Price/Earnings Ratio helps investors determine which stock is a better value.

Price Oscillator (PO): This momentum oscillator, almost identical to MACD, generates buy and sell signals when moving averages diverge and converge.

Price Rate of Change (ROC): This momentum oscillator acts as an overbought or oversold indicator for individual stocks.

Relative Strength Comparison (RSC): This indicator compares a stock's performance with a specific index to determine its relative strength or weakness.

Relative Strength Index (RSI): A momentum indicator, RSI is used to determine overbought or oversold conditions.

Stochastics: This momentum indicator is used to determine overbought and oversold conditions.

Williams %R: The Williams %R momentum indicator is used to determine overbought and oversold conditions.

Note: For further information on any of the above indicators, consult the educational sections of www.stockcharts.com, www.investopedia.com, www.barchart.com, or www.decision point.com, to name only a few.

INDICATORS AT A GLANCE

The most popular indicators are listed below with buy and sell guidelines, but keep in mind these are only guidelines, not actionable trades or fixed rules. As the market changes, the numbers sometimes change, too.

Important: Always use other indicators to confirm before buying or selling.

American Association of Individual Investors

- **Buy:** When AAII members are over 50 percent bearish, you may buy. At 60 or 70 percent, it's a screaming buy.
- **Sell:** When AAII members are over 60 percent bullish, you may sell. At 70 percent, it's a screaming sell.

Investors Intelligence Advisor Sentiment Survey

- **Buy:** When independent financial newsletter writers are over 50 percent bearish, you may buy. At 60 percent, it's a screaming buy.
- **Sell:** When independent financial newsletter writers are over 50 percent bullish, you may sell. At 60 percent, it's a screaming sell.

CBOE Put/Call Ratio

- **Buy:** An equity Put/Call Ratio higher than 1.0 (more puts are being bought) is a buy signal. Higher than 1.20 is a screaming buy.
- **Sell:** An equity Put/Call Ratio lower than 0.75 (more calls are being bought) is a sell signal. Less than 0.50 is a screaming sell.

ISEE Call/Put Ratio

- **Buy:** When the "All Equities Only" Call/Put Ratio is under 100 (more puts are being bought), it's a buy signal. Under 65 is a screaming buy.
- **Sell:** When the "All Equities Only" Call/Put Ratio is over 250 (more calls are being bought), it's a sell signal. Over 350 is a screaming sell.

The VIX

- **Buy:** When the VIX hits 40, there is panic in the options world, so you consider buying. If it goes over 50, the market could be near a bottom.
- **Sell:** When the VIX goes under 20, option traders are relatively calm. If the VIX goes below 12, option traders are too bullish, so you consider selling. The market could be near a top.

New High–New Low

- **Bullish:** If the New High–New Low is positive (new highs surpass new lows), market breadth is bullish.
- **Bearish:** If the New High–New Low is negative (new lows surpass new highs), market breadth is bearish.

Arms Index (TRIN)

- **Buy:** If the Arms Index goes above 2.0 on the close, this could be a signal to buy. Above 4.0 (possible panic) could be a screaming buy.
- **Sell:** If the Arms Index goes below 0.50 on the close, this is a signal to sell. Below 0.30 (overexuberance) could be a screaming sell.

Advance-Decline Line

- **Bullish:** When advancing stocks outnumber declining stocks (the line is rising), it is a bullish signal.
- **Bearish:** When declining stocks outnumber advancing stocks (the line is falling), it is a bearish signal.

Moving Averages

- **Buy:** If the index or stock crosses above the 50-day or 200-day moving average, that could be a signal to buy.
- **Sell:** If the index or stock crosses below the 50-day or 200-day moving average, that could be a signal to sell.

MACD

- **Buy:** When the MACD line crosses above the zero line, that could be a signal to buy.
- **Sell:** When the MACD line crosses below the zero line, that could be a signal to sell.
- **Buy:** When the MACD line crosses above the 9-day signal line (red or dashed line), that could be a signal to buy.
- **Sell:** When the MACD line crosses below the 9-day signal line, that could be a signal to sell.

Bollinger Bands

- **Overbought:** When the market (or stock) price pierces the upper band, that's an indication that the security is overbought.
- **Oversold:** When the market (or stock) price pierces the lower band, that's an indication that the security is oversold.

Relative Strength Index

- **Overbought:** If the RSI line rises above 70, that's an overbought signal.
- **Oversold:** If the RSI line drops below 30, that's an oversold signal.

Stochastics

- **Overbought:** If the slower %D line (black line) rises above 80, look for an opportunity to sell.
- **Oversold:** If the slower %D line drops below 20, look for an opportunity to buy.

THE CLOSING

All Signals Are Go!

WHAT'S NEXT?

Now that we've come to the end of our journey, it's up to you what to do next. You may want to create a link on your desktop so that you can open up your favorite indicators with a quick click of your mouse. Or you may want to do more research or experiment with the default settings. Or perhaps you will create your own indicators.

And yet, I don't want to leave you with the impression that all you need to be successful are tools and software. Not surprisingly, the stock market continues to change dramatically. The market has always been about survival, and some people will do almost anything to win, another reason why trading is such a challenging activity.

Obviously, you haven't learned everything you need to know about indicators, but at least this is a starting point. As you put down this book and start a new journey, remember that trading is not an easy endeavor; however, armed with powerful indicators and up-to-date information, you *can* be profitable. Prepare yourself emotionally for a tough battle, maintain a contrarian attitude, and trade with the odds in your favor.

No matter what you decide, I hope you come back and visit on occasion. Although some indicators will come and go, and some will be killed off as the market changes, the advice contained in this book should stand the test of time.

I want to thank you for taking the time to read my book. If even one indicator has made or saved you money, I'd be happy for you. And even more important to me, I hope I motivated you to keep learning more about indicators.

Good luck, and I wish you great success.

HOW TO CONTACT ME

I take full responsibility for all errors in this book, but let me know if you find any, so I can make changes in future editions. Feel free to write me at msincere@gmail.com if you have any questions, or visit my Web site at www.michaelsincere.com.

I'm always delighted to hear from you.

ACKNOWLEDGMENTS

Thanks to Siranirin Rattananiphon, for her devotion and support.

Thanks, too, to Jennifer Ashkenazy, my editor at McGraw-Hill, for patiently working with me until we found an idea that worked, and then helping me to see it through to completion.

I am grateful to Harvey Small, Anna Ridolfo, Laura Stangoni, Ron Weisberg, Joanne Pessin, Barbara Winther-Hansen, and Luigi Silvestri for listening; also to Paula Florez, my assistant, for helping me make the deadline; Aric Egmont for suggesting the article that prompted this book; Toni Turner for the encouragement and guidance she provided; Pascal Willain for answering questions until the last day; Kathleen Sherman, Alison Levy, and Adam Banker for their behind-the-scenes help; Web designer Ryan Saunders; graphic artist Evrice Cornelius; cartoonist Randy Ruether; author Mark Wolfinger; Laura Libretti for her wise suggestions about the publishing world; Peter McCurdy and Jane Palmieri of McGraw-Hill for their superb production and editing skills; Jonathan Burton of MarketWatch.com for the writing opportunities; Steva Kail for pointing me in the right direction; and Bertram Silverman, who I never properly thanked, for his astute observations about my life.

Thanks to the elderly couple who approached me at the mall, searching for an answer to this question: "What's the market going to do next?" Finally, I have an answer.

I don't know how to adequately express gratitude to the experts who were willing to share what they knew about market indicators. Without their help, this book could not have been written, and I can't possibly thank them enough (in alphabetical order): Gerald Appel, Richard Arms, Bernard Baumohl, John Bollinger, Michael Burke, Tony Carrion, Michael Covel, Tom DeMark, Richard Dickson, Dr. Alexander Elder, Alan Farley, Ken Fisher, Shah Gilani, Fred Hickey, Jeffrey Hirsch, Michael Kahn, Marty Kearny, Donald Keim, Bill Luby, Peter Lynch, Tom McClellan,

Gregory Morris, William J. O'Neil, Tim Ord, Martin Pring, Chris Puplava, Linda Raschke, Charles Rotblut, Richard Sipley, Jeffrey Soule, Kate Stalter, Brett Steenbarger, Kent Thacker, Dr. Van Tharp, Wayne Thorp, Toni Turner, Pascal Willain, and Larry Williams.

INDEX

ABOUT THE AUTHOR

Michael Sincere is the author of a number of investment and trading books, including *Understanding Stocks* (McGraw-Hill, 2003) and the bestselling *Understanding Options* (McGraw-Hill, 2006) to name just a few.

As a financial journalist, Sincere has written hundreds of columns and magazine articles on investing and trading, including a monthly column for MarketWatch on market indicators. He has been interviewed on dozens of national radio programs and has appeared on several financial news programs such as CNBC and ABC's *World News Now!* to talk about his books.

Sincere also finished his first novel, *The Last Au Pair*, about the exciting adventures of a group of European au pairs living in Florida. The book will be prereleased on Kindle, Nook, and Apple in January 2011.